GEORGE SEFERIS

COLLECTED POEMS

PRINCETON UNIVERSITY PRESS
IS PROUD TO INCLUDE

George Seferis: Collected Poems
*Revised Edition*

in two of its established series:

PRINCETON MODERN GREEK STUDIES
THE LOCKERT LIBRARY OF POETRY IN
TRANSLATION

The lists of titles in these series appear
on the last printed pages of this book.

PRINCETON MODERN GREEK STUDIES

THE LOCKERT LIBRARY OF POETRY
IN TRANSLATION

# GEORGE SEFERIS

# Collected Poems

TRANSLATED, EDITED, AND INTRODUCED BY
EDMUND KEELEY AND PHILIP SHERRARD

*Revised Edition*

PRINCETON UNIVERSITY PRESS
Princeton and Oxford

Published by Princeton University Press
41 William Street, Princeton, New Jersey 08540
99 Banbury Road, Oxford OX2 6JX

First published by Princeton University Press in 1995
New paperback edition, 2024
Paper ISBN 9780691264660
ISBN (e-book) 9780691264677

The Library of Congress has cataloged the previous edition as follows:

Seferis, George,1900-1971.
[Poems. English]
Collected poems I George Seferis; translated, edited. and inrtoduced by Edmund Keeley
and Philip Sherrard. - Rev. ed.
p. cm. -(Lockert library of poetry in translation) (Princeton modern Greek studies)
Includes bibliograhical references (p. ) and index. ISBN 0-691-06861-5 (CL). -
ISBN 0-691-01491-4 (PB)
I. Seferis, George, 1900–1971 -Tranlations into English.    I. Keeley, Edmund.
II. Sherrard, Philip.    III. Title.    IV. Series    V. Series: Princeton modern Greek
studies.

PA5610.S36A24  1995
889'.132—<lc20                                                                92-10552

The Lockert Library of Poetry in Translation is supported by a
bequest from Charles Lacy Lockert (1888-1974).

Cover images : Roman, Antioch, Turkey, early 3rd century C.E., *Mosaic pavement:
drinking contest of Herakles and Dionysos*. Stone and glass, 526 x 527 cm,
229.2 x 295.5 cm (figural scene). Gift of the Committee for the Excavation of
Antioch to Princeton University. Greek pattern from Radiocat / Shutterstock

# CONTENTS

BOOK OF EXERCISES

*Poems Given*

*Mr Stratis Thalassinos*

THREE SECRET POEMS

From BOOK OF EXERCISES II

APPENDIX: *Rhymed Poems*

TURNING POINT

*Shells, Clouds*

From BOOK OF EXERCISES

# FOREWORD

THE POETRY OF George Seferis, whatever relation it may have
to the literature of other countries, stems first of all from a
tradition that is eminently Greek. This means that it not only
shares in the modern revival which has produced, during the
last hundred and fifty years or so, such distinguished Greek
poets as Solomos, Kalvos, Palamas, Sikelianos, Cavafy, Elytis
and Ritsos; it also proceeds, like most of the poetry that be-
longs to this revival, from earlier sources. One of these is the
long tradition of Greek ballads and folk songs. Both the spirit
of Greek folk literature and its dominant form, the 'dekapenta-
syllavos',[1] can be traced back directly at least to the Byzantine
period, and both have been consistently influential since that
time, though the form has naturally been modified in keeping
with new needs. Seferis's early poem, 'Erotikos Logos' (1930),
is a major example of such modification: a successful attempt to
adapt the dekapentasyllavos line to the expression of a contem-
porary sensibility.

Another area of the post-medieval poetic tradition that has
remained equally influential is the more complex and sophisti-
cated literature which developed on the island of Crete during
the sixteenth and seventeenth centuries. The dramatic literature
of Crete includes plays such as *Abraham's Sacrifice*, a religious
work, and the *Erophile*, a bloodthirsty tragedy in which all the
main characters are killed or kill themselves; but the master-
piece of this more complex (and, in contrast with the folk
ballads, more introspective) tradition is the epic romance, the
*Erotokritos*, by Vitzentzos Kornaros, a work of 10,052 verses
telling of the love of Aretousa, daughter of the king of Athens,
and the valiant Erotokritos, son of one of the leading court
families. This epic became immensely popular throughout the

---

1. A line of fifteen syllables, with a caesura after the eighth syllable and two
main accents, one on the sixth or eighth syllable and one on the fourteenth.

Greek world, great sections – and sometimes even the whole of it – being recited by heart as though an ordinary folk epic: the kind of recitation that haunts Seferis's persona in 'Reflections on a Foreign Line of Verse', where he speaks of

> ... certain old sailors of my childhood who, leaning on
>     their nets with winter coming on and the wind raging,
> used to recite, with tears in their eyes, the song of
>     Erotokritos;
> it was then I would shudder in my sleep at the unjust fate
>     of Aretousa descending the marble steps.

Seferis has written the best Greek critical commentary on the *Erotokritos*,[2] and its influence, as a monument to the poetic possibilities of the demotic Greek language,[3] is apparent from the use he makes of it in his 'Erotikos Logos', where he introduces actual phrases from the epic into the text of his poem in order to establish an analogy between his diction and that of another vital, relevant moment in his nation's literary past.

Cretan literature of the sixteenth and seventeenth centuries and the folk tradition are, then, among the more important local sources of Seferis's art, particularly because of their creative exploitation of the Greek language; at the same time, however, the poetry of Seferis and that of his immediate predecessors differs in an important respect from the poetry of both these literatures: in the use made of images, characters and myths that derive from ancient Greece. Whether it is Palamas contrasting the 'people of relics' – who reign among the temples and olive groves of the Attic landscape – with the modern crowd crawling along sluggishly, like a caterpillar over a white flower (in *Life Immovable*); or Cavafy evoking – perhaps ironically, perhaps erotically – some scene out of his poetic world of ancient Alexandria; or Sikelianos endeavouring

---

2. Included in his Δοκιμές [Essays], Athens, 1974.

3. Demotic Greek, as opposed to purist Greek (known as *katharevousa*), is now the literary language of modern Greece, though it was not generally accepted as such until this century.

to resurrect the whole pantheon of the ancient gods and to be a
hierophant to their mysteries; or Seferis searching for the arch-
aic king of Asini – the substantial man who fought with heroes
– and finding only the unsubstantial void of contemporary
existence; whichever it is, the ancient world in all its aspects
preoccupies the imagination of these poets constantly. This
preoccupation is only natural in a country which, like Greece,
remains full of the physical remnants of antiquity; everywhere
reminders of the ancient past leap to the eye and stimulate the
mind:

> Scattered drums of a Doric column
> Razed to the ground
> By unexpected earthquakes

as Sikelianos puts it in 'The Conscience of Personal Creative-
ness', or, to quote Seferis himself: 'fragments of a life which
was once complete, disturbing fragments, close to us, ours for
one moment, and then mysterious and unapproachable as the
lines of a stone licked smooth by the wave or of a shell in the
sea's depths.'[4] This means that the Greek poet who draws on
classical mythology in shaping the drama of his verse enjoys a
large advantage over his similarly disposed contemporaries in
England or America: he can evoke characters and settings that
have mythological overtones with less danger of being merely
literary in doing so, with less danger of arbitrarily imposing
gods and heroes on an alien landscape – Tiresias on the Thames
or Prometheus in Pennsylvania, for example – since his own
natural landscape is that to which these gods and heroes them-
selves once belonged and in which they still confront the
mind's eye plausibly.

Seferis, like most poets of modern Greece, has fully ex-
ploited this advantage. His secret (in addition to his advantage)
is that he always offers an appropriate setting – a poetically

---

4. From *Delphi*, translated by Philip Sherrard, Munich and Ahrbeck, Han-
over, 1963, p. 8.

realistic setting – before he allows any legendary figures to
appear on his stage; before he attempts to carry the reader to
the level of myth, he earns his sympathy and belief by convin-
cingly representing the present reality sustaining his myth –
and it is a contemporary, Greek reality always. In this way the
myth comes to life fully, the ancient and modern worlds meet
in a metaphor without strain or contrivance as we find the
legendary figures moving anachronistically onto the contem-
porary stage that the poet has set before our eyes. The anachro-
nism is, of course, very much to the point: in one sense, what
was then is now, but in another sense, what is now was then;
the modern voyager, for instance, shares something of Odys-
seus's fate, while Odysseus finds a symbolic representation of
his fate in the modern setting that the poet has him confront:
the deserted, arid, repetitious land and the calm, embittering
sea so frequently encountered in Seferis's poetry are symbolic
of Odysseus's frustrating voyage, of his failure to realize the
island paradise he longs for. And his fate is that of every
wanderer seeking a final harbour, a spiritual fulfilment, that he
can't seem to reach. The frustrations of the wanderer are per-
ennial; as Seferis puts it in an illuminating commentary on the
rôle of mythic characters in his verse: '... men of inconstancy,
of wanderings and of wars, though they differ and may change
in terms of greatness and value... always move among the
same monsters and the same longings. So we keep the symbols
and the names that the myth has brought down to us, realizing
as we do so that the typical characters have changed in keeping
with the passing of time and the different conditions of our
world – which are none other than the conditions of everyone
who seeks expression.'[5]

The mythology of the ancient world thus plays a crucial rôle
in Seferis, but it would be a mistake to regard this source in
isolation, since all the various threads of the Greek tradition

5. From '"Ενα γράμμα γιὰ τὴν «Κίχλη»' [A Letter on *'Thrush'*],
'Αγγλο-ελληνικὴ 'Επιθεώρηση, IV (July–August 1950), 501–6.

that we have mentioned here – folk, literary and mythic – are tightly woven together in his work; one senses really the whole of the Greek past, as it is represented in poetry from the age of Homer down to the contemporary period, behind Seferis's maturest verse, giving it overtones and undertones sometimes too subtle for the non-Greek ear to catch (especially when they have to be caught in a language foreign to the text). But even as one does catch the sound of a richly traditional voice, a voice learned in the best poetry of previous ages, one is also aware that the voice is very much of the present age and that the poet's sensibility couldn't be farther from that of an antiquarian delving nostalgically into the past in order to escape from the bewilderments and afflictions of modern life: the past is always there to shape and illuminate an image of the present. And if this image seems inevitably to have its sorrow – that 'καημός τῆς Ρωμιοσύνης' which is so specifically Greek that Seferis rightly regards any translation of the phrase as a distortion – one can take it simply for an index of the image's veracity, since a mature consciousness in the Greek world cannot but be aware of how much this world has achieved only to find everything suddenly ruined by the 'war, destruction, exile' of constantly unpropitious times, as Seferis's persona puts it in 'Thrush' – aware of how much and how little individual creative effort signifies in a world so vulnerable. It is the depth of this awareness, so often incomprehensible to nations with shorter and less tragic histories or with more superficial memories, that serves him for protection against those too-easily won positions, that too-readily assumed despair, from which much modern poetry issues.

If Seferis's sensibility has always been too specifically Greek to allow the easy sharing of what he himself has called 'the "Waste Land" feeling' that was common to Anglo-American and European poets after the First World War,[6] his expression

---

6. In 'Letter to a Foreign Friend' (included in Rex Warner's translation of Seferis's essays, On the Greek Style, Athens, 1982).

of this sensibility has been influenced by the example of several poets outside the Greek tradition. There is no doubt, for instance, that in the early phase of his career Seferis was keenly interested in the tonal and stylistic experiments of his French contemporaries, and, indeed, often seemed to be striving for a 'pure' poetry in the manner of Valéry. With the appearance of *Mythistorema* in 1935, a distinct change in style became evident, in part the consequence of the poet's sympathetic reading of Eliot and Pound during the early thirties and in part the last phase of a personal stylistic catharsis that had already begun to show in *The Cistern* (1932). With *Mythistorema*, Seferis abandoned the relatively formal mode of his earlier volumes in favour of the much freer and more natural mode that is characteristic of all his mature poetry,[7] where we inevitably find a precisely controlled style, undecorated by embellishment, the colouring always primary and the imagery sparse. In this mature poetry Seferis also combines the modes of everyday speech with the forms and rhythms of traditional usage in a way that creates the effect of both density and economy – an effect almost impossible to reproduce in English, however carefully one may attempt to duplicate the particular character of the poet's style.

But if one discerns the influence of foreign sources in Seferis's stylistic development, one also discerns that the substance of his poetry has remained consistently individual since the start: in the finest poems of each of his volumes (often those least accessible to the Western reader because the least mythological or 'classicist'), there is always that tragic sense of life which comes most forcefully out of a direct, personal experience of history – out of a poet *engagé* responding to what he has known and felt of human suffering, or at least what he has clearly seen of it at close quarters. This is not merely to repeat

7. We have chosen to open this collected edition with the poems in which Seferis's mature voice is first heard rather than with the poems of his less characteristic – and less translatable – early phase (see note to 'Rhymed Poems', p. 308).

the frequently suggested relationship, for example, between Seferis's poetic representation of exile and his actual exile after the loss of his childhood home in the Asia Minor disaster of 1922 and during his many years away from Greece in his country's diplomatic service, valid though this relationship may be in some respects; more important, perhaps, than his capacity to make the personal poetic in this way is his capacity to capture the metaphoric significance of some event that has moved him, his capacity to transform a personal experience or insight into a metaphor that defines the character of our times: for example, the metaphor of that 'presentable and quiet' man who walks along weeping in 'Narration', the 'instrument of a boundless pain / that's finally lost all significance'; or the couple at the end of 'The Last Day' who go home to turn on the light because they are sick of walking in the dusk; or the messengers in 'Our Sun' who arrive, dirty and breathless, to die with only one intelligible sentence on their lips: 'We don't have time' (all of these poems written, incidentally, either just before or just after the outbreak of the Second World War in Europe). These are the kind of metaphors that project Seferis's vision beyond any strictly local or strictly personal history and that bring to the mind's eye images as definitive, as universal, as any offered by the poetry of Seferis's contemporaries in Europe and America.

There are also moments when an event that would seem to be only of local or personal significance becomes the occasion for a simple statement of truth about human experience – a statement more direct, and sometimes more precise, than the poet's metaphoric mode allows: the second stanza of 'Last Stop', written on the eve of Seferis's return to Greece at the end of the Second World War, is an occasion of this kind, as is the conclusion of 'Helen', written during the Cyprus conflict of the early 1950s. It is moments such as these, when the poet describes the corruption of war in a voice made wise and simple by the clearest vision, that raise his poems about specific historical events far above the level of political comment or propaganda and that show him to have sustained – through his poems about the Second World War and his volume dedicated to the people of Cyprus – the same universalizing sensibility that has shaped his image of contemporary history since *Myth-istorema* and several earlier poems that anticipate it. The distinguishing attribute of Seferis's genius – one that he shares with Yeats and Eliot – was always his ability to make out of a local politics, out of a personal history or mythology, some sort of general statement or metaphor; his long Odyssean voyage on rotten timbers to those islands ever slightly out of reach has the same force of definitive, general insight that we find in Yeats's voyage to Byzantium or Eliot's journey over desert country to a fragmentary salvation. Seferis's politics are never simply the restricted politics of a nationalist – though he was very much a 'national' poet in his choice of themes, and though his vision is often rendered in those terms that best characterize his nation: its landscape, its literature, its historical and mythic past. His politics are those of the poet with an especially acute sensitivity to issues that are not restricted simply to contemporary history. Though he was preoccupied with his tradition as few other poets of the same generation were with theirs, and though he had long been engaged, directly and actively, in the immediate political aspirations of his nation, his value as a poet lies in what he made of this preoccupation and this engagement in fashioning a broad poetic vision – in offering insights that carry with them the weight of universal truths and that thus serve to reveal the deeper meaning of human existence.

This new edition of George Seferis's collected poems contains translations of all the poems that Seferis published during his lifetime. We have included three poems that were serially published by Seferis before his death in 1971 but which were first collected in the posthumous volume entitled *Book of Exercises II*. Most of the poems that make up that volume are omitted here for the reasons we give in our third, expanded edition of the bilingual *Collected Poems*, published in 1981.

Since that date the number of studies of Seferis's work has so multiplied, and is being so continuously augmented, that we have decided to exclude them from the brief bibliography. Our notes remain as they were: readers who wish for further information referring to the Greek text should consult the Ikaros (Athens) edition of Seferis's poems, edited by George Savidis. We have only to add that this new collection incorporates many revisions of the translations that appeared in our 1981 edition. In fact, we would like to think that this revised volume contains our definitive English versions of virtually all of Seferis's poetry. We would also like to think that the volume bears witness both to the full scope of the poet's vision and to the fineness of the artistry with which this vision is expressed.

E. K.
P. S.

# ACKNOWLEDGEMENT

As WAS INDICATED in our first collected edition of Seferis's poetry (1967), our work was facilitated at the start by Mr Seferis's generous interest and cooperation. The serial publication of a number of the translations in their earliest form is acknowledged in the first edition, as is the republication of selections from our initial collaborative enterprise, identified here in the Bibliographical Note. Those poems that have been revised for the current edition appear here in their revised form for the first time.

A diamond at the foot of a page indicates that the end of an irregular stanza or verse-paragraph has coincided with the end of a page: there would otherwise have been a line-space. Diamonds do not appear in those poems that have a regular stanza pattern.

# Mythistorema

Si j'ai du *goût*, ce n'est guères
Que pour la terre et les pierres.

— ARTHUR RIMBAUD

# Mythistorema

### 1

The angel –
three years we waited for him, attention riveted,
closely scanning
the pines the shore the stars.
One with the blade of the plough or the ship's keel
we were searching to find once more the first seed
so that the age-old drama could begin again.

We returned to our homes broken,
limbs incapable, mouths cracked
by the taste of rust and brine.
When we woke we travelled towards the north, strangers
plunged into mist by the immaculate wings of swans that
  wounded us.
On winter nights the strong wind from the east maddened
  us,
in the summers we were lost in the agony of days that
  couldn't die.

We brought back
these carved reliefs of a humble art.

## 2

Still one more well inside a cave.
It used to be easy for us to draw up idols and ornaments
to please those friends who still remained loyal to us.

The ropes have broken; only the grooves on the well's lip
remind us of our past happiness:
the fingers on the rim, as the poet put it.
The fingers feel the coolness of the stone a little,
then the body's fever prevails over it
and the cave stakes its soul and loses it
every moment, full of silence, without a drop of water.

3

*Remember the baths where you were murdered*

I woke with this marble head in my hands;
it exhausts my elbows and I don't know where to put it
     down.
It was falling into the dream as I was coming out of the
     dream
so our life became one and it will be very difficult for it to
     separate again.

I look at the eyes: neither open nor closed
I speak to the mouth which keeps trying to speak
I hold the cheeks which have broken through the skin.
That's all I'm able to do.

My hands disappear and come towards me
mutilated.

4

*Argonauts*

And a soul
if it is to know itself
must look
into its own soul:
the stranger and enemy, we've seen him in the mirror.

They were good, the companions, they didn't complain
about the work or the thirst or the frost,
they had the bearing of trees and waves
that accept the wind and the rain
accept the night and the sun
without changing in the midst of change.
They were fine, whole days
they sweated at the oars with lowered eyes
breathing in rhythm
and their blood reddened a submissive skin.
Sometimes they sang, with lowered eyes
as we were passing the deserted island with the Barbary figs
to the west, beyond the cape of the dogs
that bark.
If it is to know itself, they said
it must look into its own soul, they said
and the oars struck the sea's gold
in the sunset.
We went past many capes many islands the sea
leading to another sea, gulls and seals.
Sometimes disconsolate women wept
lamenting their lost children
and others frantic sought Alexander the Great
and glories buried in the depths of Asia.

We moored on shores full of night-scents,
the birds singing, with waters that left on the hands
the memory of a great happiness.
But the voyages did not end.
Their souls became one with the oars and the oarlocks
with the solemn face of the prow
with the rudder's wake
with the water that shattered their image.
The companions died one by one,
with lowered eyes. Their oars
mark the place where they sleep on the shore.

No one remembers them. Justice.

5

We didn't know them
                    deep down it was hope that said
we'd known them since early childhood.
We saw them perhaps twice and then they took to the ships:
cargoes of coal, cargoes of grain, and our friends
lost beyond the ocean forever.
Dawn finds us beside the tired lamp
drawing on paper, awkwardly, painfully,
ships mermaids or sea shells;
at dusk we go down to the river
because it shows us the way to the sea;
and we spend the nights in cellars that smell of tar.

Our friends have left us
                    perhaps we never saw them, perhaps
we met them when sleep
still brought us close to the breathing wave
perhaps we search for them because we search for the other
        life,
beyond the statues.

6

*M. R.*

The garden with its fountains in the rain
you will see only from behind the clouded glass
of the low window. Your room
will be lit only by the flames from the fireplace
and sometimes the distant lightning will reveal
the wrinkles on your forehead, my old Friend.

The garden with the fountains that in your hands
was a rhythm of the other life, beyond the broken
statues and the tragic columns
and a dance among the oleanders
near the new quarries –
misty glass will have cut it off from your life.
You won't breathe; earth and the sap of the trees
will spring from your memory to strike
this window struck by rain
from the outside world.

7

*South wind*

Westward the sea merges with a mountain range.
From our left the south wind blows and drives us mad,
the kind of wind that strips bones of their flesh.
Our house among pines and carobs.
Large windows. Large tables
for writing you the letters we've been writing
so many months now, dropping them
into the space between us in order to fill it up.

Star of dawn, when you lowered your eyes
our hours were sweeter than oil
on a wound, more joyful than cold water
to the palate, more peaceful than a swan's wings.
You held our life in the palm of your hand.
After the bitter bread of exile,
at night if we remain in front of the white wall
your voice approaches us like the hope of fire;
and again this wind hones
a razor against our nerves.

Each of us writes you the same thing
and each falls silent in the other's presence,
watching, each of us, the same world separately
the light and darkness on the mountain range
and you.
Who will lift this sorrow from our hearts?
Yesterday evening a heavy rain and again today
the covered sky burdens us. Our thoughts –
like the pine needles of yesterday's downpour

bunched up and useless in front of our doorway –
would build a collapsing tower.

Among these decimated villages
on this promontory, open to the south wind
with the mountain range in front of us hiding you,
who will appraise for us the sentence to oblivion?
Who will accept our offering, at this close of autumn?

8

What are they after, our souls, travelling
on the decks of decayed ships
crowded in with sallow women and crying babies
unable to forget themselves either with the flying fish
or with the stars that the masts point out at their tips;
grated by gramophone records
committed to non-existent pilgrimages unwillingly
murmuring broken thoughts from foreign languages.

What are they after, our souls, travelling
on rotten brine-soaked timbers
from harbour to harbour?

Shifting broken stones, breathing in
the pine's coolness with greater difficulty each day,
swimming in the waters of this sea
and of that sea,
without the sense of touch
without men
in a country that is no longer ours
nor yours.

We knew that the islands were beautiful
somewhere round about here where we grope,
slightly lower down or slightly higher up,
a tiny space.

9

The harbour is old, I can't wait any longer
for the friend who left for the island with the pine trees
for the friend who left for the island with the plane trees
for the friend who left for the open sea.
I stroke the rusted cannons, I stroke the oars
so that my body may revive and decide.
The sails give off only the smell
of salt from the other storm.

If I chose to remain alone, what I longed for
was solitude, not this kind of waiting,
my soul shattered on the horizon,
these lines, these colours, this silence.

The night's stars take me back to Odysseus,
to his anticipation of the dead among the asphodels.
When we moored here we hoped to find among the
    asphodels
the gorge that knew the wounded Adonis.

10

Our country is closed in, all mountains
that day and night have the low sky as their roof.
We have no rivers, we have no wells, we have no springs,
only a few cisterns – and these empty – that echo, and that
      we worship.
A stagnant hollow sound, the same as our loneliness
the same as our love, the same as our bodies.
We find it strange that once we were able to build
our houses, huts and sheep-folds.
And our marriages, the cool coronals and the fingers,
become enigmas inexplicable to our soul.
How were our children born, how did they grow strong?

Our country is closed in. The two black Symplegades
close it in. When we go down
to the harbours on Sunday to breathe freely
we see, lit in the sunset,
the broken planks from voyages that never ended,
bodies that no longer know how to love.

11

Sometimes your blood froze like the moon
in the limitless night your blood
spread its white wings over
the black rocks, the shapes of trees and houses,
with a little light from our childhood years.

12

*Bottle in the sea*

Three rocks, a few burnt pines, a lone chapel
and farther above
the same landscape repeated starts again:
three rocks in the shape of a gateway, rusted,
a few burnt pines, black and yellow,
and a square hut buried in whitewash;
and still farther above, many times over,
the same landscape recurs level after level
to the horizon, to the twilit sky.

Here we moored the ship to splice the broken oars,
to drink water and to sleep.
The sea that embittered us is deep and unexplored
and unfolds a boundless calm.
Here among the pebbles we found a coin
and threw dice for it.
The youngest won it and disappeared.

We put to sea again with our broken oars.

13

*Hydra*

Dolphins banners and the sound of cannons.
The sea once so bitter to your soul
bore the many-coloured and glittering ships
it swayed, rolled and tossed them, all blue with white wings,
once so bitter to your soul
now full of colours in the sun.

White sails and sunlight and wet oars
struck with a rhythm of drums on stilled waves.

Your eyes, watching, would be beautiful,
your arms, reaching out, would glow,
your lips would come alive, as they used to,
at such a miracle:
that's what you were looking for
                what were you looking for in front of ashes
or in the rain in the fog in the wind
even when the lights were growing dim
and the city was sinking and on the stone pavement
the Nazarene showed you his heart,
what were you looking for? why don't you come? what
    were you looking for?

14

Three red pigeons in the light
inscribing our fate in the light
with colours and gestures of people
we once loved.

15

*Quid πλατανὼν opacissimus?*

Sleep wrapped you in green leaves like a tree
you breathed like a tree in the quiet light
in the limpid spring I looked at your face:
eyelids closed, eyelashes brushing the water.
In the soft grass my fingers found your fingers
I held your pulse a moment
and felt elsewhere your heart's pain.

Under the plane tree, near the water, among laurel
sleep moved you and scattered you
around me, near me, without my being able to touch the
    whole of you –
one as you were with your silence;
seeing your shadow grow and diminish,
lose itself in the other shadows, in the other
world that let you go yet held you back.

The life that they gave us to live, we lived.
Pity those who wait with such patience
lost in the black laurel under the heavy plane trees
and those, alone, who speak to cisterns and wells
and drown in the voice's circles.
Pity the companion who shared our privation and our sweat
and plunged into the sun like a crow beyond the ruins,
without hope of enjoying our reward.

Give us, outside sleep, serenity.

16

*The name is Orestes*

On the track, once more on the track, on the track,
how many times around, how many blood-stained laps,
    how many black
rows; the people who watch me,
who watched me when, in the chariot,
I raised my hand glorious, and they roared triumphantly.

The froth of the horses strikes me, when will the horses tire?
The axle creaks, the axle burns, when will the axle burst
    into flame?
When will the reins break, when will the hooves
tread flush on the ground
on the soft grass, among the poppies
where, in the spring, you picked a daisy.
They were lovely, your eyes, but you didn't know where
    to look
nor did I know where to look, I, without a country,
I who go on struggling here, how many times around?
and I feel my knees give way over the axle
over the wheels, over the wild track
knees buckle easily when the gods so will it,
no one can escape, what use is strength, you can't
escape the sea that cradled you and that you search for
at this time of trial, with the horses panting,
with the reeds that used to sing in autumn to the Lydian
    mode
the sea you cannot find no matter how you run
no matter how you circle past the black, bored Eumenides,
unforgiven.

17

*Astyanax*

Now that you are leaving, take the boy with you as well,
the boy who saw the light under that plane tree,
one day when trumpets resounded and weapons shone
and the sweating horses
bent to the trough to touch with wet nostrils
the green surface of the water.

The olive trees with the wrinkles of our fathers
the rocks with the wisdom of our fathers
and our brother's blood alive on the earth
were a vital joy, a rich pattern
for the souls who knew their prayer.

Now that you are leaving, now that the day of payment
dawns, now that no one knows
whom he will kill and how he will die,
take with you the boy who saw the light
under the leaves of that plane tree
and teach him to study the trees.

18

I regret having let a broad river slip through my fingers
without drinking a single drop.
Now I'm sinking into the stone.
A small pine tree in the red soil
is all the company I have.
Whatever I loved vanished with the houses
that were new last summer
and crumbled in the winds of autumn.

19

Even if the wind blows it doesn't cool us
and the shade is meagre under the cypress trees
and all around slopes ascending to the mountains;

they're a burden for us
the friends who no longer know how to die.

20

In my breast the wound opens again
when the stars descend and become kin to my body
when silence falls under the footsteps of men.

These stones sinking into time, how far will they drag me
    with them?
The sea, the sea, who will be able to drain it dry?
I see the hands beckon each dawn to the vulture and the
    hawk
bound as I am to the rock that suffering has made mine,
I see the trees breathing the black serenity of the dead
and then the smiles, so static, of the statues.

21

We who set out on this pilgrimage
looked at the broken statues
became distracted and said that life is not so easily lost
that death has unexplored paths
and its own particular justice;

that while we, still upright on our feet, are dying,
affiliated in stone
united in hardness and weakness,
the ancient dead have escaped the circle and risen again
and smile in a strange silence.

22

So very much having passed before our eyes
that even our eyes saw nothing, but beyond
and behind was memory like the white sheet one night in an
    enclosure
where we saw strange visions, even stranger than you,
pass by and vanish into the motionless foliage of a pepper
    tree;

having known this fate of ours so well
wandering among broken stones, three or six thousand years
searching in collapsed buildings that might have been our
    homes
trying to remember dates and heroic deeds:
will we be able?

having been bound and scattered,
having struggled, as they said, with non-existent difficulties
lost, then finding again a road full of blind regiments
sinking in marshes and in the lake of Marathon,
will we be able to die as we should?

23

A little farther
we will see the almond trees blossoming
the marble gleaming in the sun
the sea breaking into waves

a little farther,
let us rise a little higher.

24

Here end the works of the sea, the works of love.
Those who will some day live here where we end –
should the blood happen to darken in their memory and
    overflow –
let them not forget us, the weak souls among the asphodels,
let them turn the heads of the victims towards Erebus:

We who had nothing will school them in serenity.


*December 1933–December 1934*

# Gymnopaidia

Santorini is geologically composed of pumice stone
and china clay; in her bay ... islands have appeared
and disappeared. This island was once the centre of
a very ancient religion. The lyrical dances, with a
strict and heavy rhythm, performed here were called:
Gymnopaidia.

*– Guide to Greece*

# Gymnopaidia

## I  SANTORINI

Bend if you can to the dark sea forgetting
the sound of a flute on naked feet
that trod your sleep in the other, the sunken life.

Write if you can on your last shell
the day the name the place
and fling it into the sea so that it sinks.

Naked we found ourselves on the pumice-stone
watching the rising islands
watching the red islands sink
into their sleep, into our sleep.
Here naked we found ourselves, holding
the scales that tilted towards
injustice.

Heel of power, barefaced will, calculated love,
schemes that ripen in the midday sun,
course of fate with a new hand
striking the shoulder;
in the land that was scattered, that can't bear any more,
in the land that was once our land
the islands – rust and ash – are sinking.

Altars destroyed
and friends forgotten
leaves of the palm tree in mud.

Let your hands travel, if you can,
here on time's curve with the ship
that touched the horizon.
When the dice struck the flagstone
when the lance struck the breast-plate
when the eye recognized the stranger
and love went dry
in punctured souls;
when looking round you see
feet harvested everywhere
dead hands everywhere
eyes darkened everywhere;
when you can't any longer choose
even the death you wanted as your own –
hearing a cry,
even the wolf's cry,
your due:
let your hands travel, if you can,
free yourself from unfaithful time
and sink –
whoever raises the great stones sinks.

## II   MYCENAE

Give me your hands, give me your hands, give me your
    hands.

I have seen in the night
the sharp peak of the mountain,
seen the plain beyond flooded
with the light of an invisible moon,
seen, turning my head,
black stones huddled
and my life taut as a chord
beginning and end
the final moment:
my hands.

Whoever raises the great stones sinks;
I've raised these stones as long as I was able
I've loved these stones as long as I was able
these stones, my fate.
Wounded by my own soil
tortured by my own shirt
condemned by my own gods,
these stones.

I know that they don't know, but I
who've followed so many times
the path from killer to victim
from victim to punishment
from punishment to the next murder,
groping
the inexhaustible purple
that night of the return
when the Furies began whistling

in the meagre grass –
I've seen snakes crossed with vipers
knotted over the evil generation
our fate.

Voices out of the stone out of sleep
deeper here where the world darkens,
memory of toil rooted in the rhythm
beaten upon the earth by feet
forgotten.
Bodies sunk into the foundations
of the other time, naked. Eyes
glued, glued to a point
that you can't make out, much as you want to:
the soul
struggling to become your own soul.

Not even the silence is now yours
here where the millstones have stopped turning.

*October 1935*

*Book of Exercises*

# POEMS GIVEN

# Letter of Mathios Paskalis

The skyscrapers of New York will never know the coolness
    that comes down on Kifisia
but when I see the two cypress trees above your familiar
    church
with the paintings of the damned being tortured in fire and
    brimstone
then I recall the two chimneys behind the cedars I used to
    like so much when I was abroad.

All through March rheumatism wracked your lovely loins
    and in summer you went to Aidipsos.
God! what a struggle it is for life to keep going, as though it
    were a swollen river passing through the eye of a
    needle.
Heavy heat till nightfall, the stars discharging midges, I
    myself drinking bitter lemonades and still remaining
    thirsty;
Moon and movies, phantoms and the suffocating
    pestiferous harbour.

Verina, life has ruined us, along with the Attic skies and the
    intellectuals clambering up their own heads
and the landscapes reduced by drought and hunger to
    posing
like young men selling their souls in order to wear a
    monocle
like young girls – sunflowers swallowing their heads so as
    to become lilies.

The days go by slowly; my own days circulate among the
    clocks dragging the second hand in tow.
Remember how we used to twist breathless through the
    alleys so as not to be gutted by the headlights of cars.
The idea of the world abroad enveloped us and closed us in
    like a net
and we left with a sharp knife hidden within us and you said
    'Harmodios and Aristogeiton'.

Verina, lower your head so that I can see you, though even
    if I were to see you I'd want to look beyond.
What's a man's value? What does he want and how will he
    justify his existence at the Second Coming?
Ah, to find myself on a derelict ship lost in the Pacific Ocean
    alone with the sea and the wind
alone and without a wireless or strength to fight the elements.

*Kokkinaras, 5 August 1928*

# Syngrou Avenue, 1930

*To George Theotokas, who discovered it*

When the smile
breathing beside you conquers you, tries to submit and
    doesn't consent

when the dizziness that remains from your wandering
    among books moves from your mind to the pepper
    trees on either side

when you leave the petrified ship travelling with broken
    rigging towards the depths
the arch with gold decoration
the columns whose burden makes them more narrow

when you leave behind you the bodies deliberately carved
    for counting and for hoarding riches
the soul that, whatever you do, doesn't match your own soul
the toll you pay
that small feminine face in the cradle shining in the sun

when you let your heart and your thought become one
with the blackish river that stretches, stiffens and goes away:

Break Ariadne's thread and look!
The blue body of the mermaid.

## Reflections on a Foreign Line of Verse

*For Elli, Christmas 1931*

Fortunate he who's made the voyage of Odysseus.
Fortunate if on setting out he's felt the rigging of a love
    strong in his body, spreading there like veins where
    the blood throbs.

A love of indissoluble rhythm, unconquerable like music
    and endless
because it was born when we were born and when we die
    whether it dies too neither we know nor does anyone else.

I ask God to help me say, at some moment of great happiness,
    what that love is;
sometimes when I sit surrounded by exile I hear its distant
    murmur like the sound of sea struck by an inexplicable
    hurricane.

And again and again the shade of Odysseus appears before
    me, his eyes red from the waves' salt,
from his ripe longing to see once more the smoke ascending
    from his warm hearth and the dog grown old waiting
    by the door.

A large man, whispering through his whitened beard words
    in our language spoken as it was three thousand years ago.
He extends a palm calloused by the ropes and the tiller, his
    skin weathered by the dry north wind, by heat and snow.
It's as if he wants to expel from among us the superhuman
    one-eyed Cyclops, the Sirens who make you forget
    with their song, Scylla and Charybdis:

so many complex monsters that prevent us from remem-
   bering that he too was a man struggling in the world
   with soul and body.

He is the mighty Odysseus: he who proposed the wooden
   horse with which the Achaeans captured Troy.
I imagine he's coming to tell me how I too may build a
   wooden horse to capture my own Troy.

Because he speaks humbly and calmly, without effort, as
   though he were my father
or certain old sailors of my childhood who, leaning on their
   nets with winter coming on and the wind raging,

used to recite, with tears in their eyes, the song of Erotokritos;
it was then I would shudder in my sleep at the unjust fate of
   Aretousa descending the marble steps.

He tells me of the harsh pain you feel when the ship's sails
   swell with memory and your soul becomes a rudder;
of being alone, dark in the night, and helpless as chaff on the
   threshing-floor;

of the bitterness of seeing your companions one by one
   pulled down into the elements and scattered;
and of how strangely you gain strength conversing with the
   dead when the living who remain no longer meet your
   need.

He speaks . . . I still see his hands that knew how to judge the
   carving of the mermaid at the prow
presenting me the waveless blue sea in the heart of winter.

## Sixteen Haiku

*Τοῦτο τὸ ἀκαριαῖον . . .* – MARCUS AURELIUS

### 1

Spill into the lake
but a drop of wine
and the sun vanishes.

### 2

In the field not one
four-leaf clover:
which of the three is to blame?

### 3

*In the Museum garden*

Empty chairs:
the statues have gone back
to the other museum.

### 4

Is it the voice
of our dead friends or
the phonograph?

5

Her fingers
against the blue scarf –
look: corals.


6

Meditative
her breasts heavy
in the looking-glass.


7

Again I put on
the tree's foliage
and you – you bleat.


8

Night, the wind
separation
spreads and undulates.


9

*Young Fate*

Naked woman
the pomegranate that broke
was full of stars.

10

Now I raise
a dead butterfly
without make-up.


11

How can you gather together
the thousand fragments
of each person?


12

*Unprofitable line*

What's wrong with the rudder?
The boat inscribes circles
and there's not a single gull.


13

*Sick Fury*

She has no eyes,
the snakes she held
devour her hands.

14

In this column a hole:
can you see
Persephone?

15

The world sinks:
hang on, it'll leave you
alone in the sun.

16

You write:
the ink grew less,
the sea increases.

This body that hoped to flower like a branch,
to bear fruit, to become a flute in the frost –
fantasy has thrust it into a noisy bee-hive
so that musical rhythm may come and torture it.

# Flight

Our love was not other than this:
it left, came back and brought us
a lowered eyelid in the far distance
a stony smile, lost
in the dawn grass
a strange shell our soul
insistently tried to explain.

Our love was not other than this: it groped
silently among the things around us
to explain why we don't want to die
so passionately.

And if we've held on by the loins, clasped
other necks as tightly as we could,
mingled our breath with the breath
of that person
if we've closed our eyes, it was not other than this:
simply that deep longing to hang on
in our flight.

## Description

She draws near with her clouded eyes, that sculptured hand
the hand that held the tiller
the hand that held the pen
the hand that opened in the wind,
everything threatens her silence.

A ripple runs from the pine trees towards the sea
plays with the breeze's humble breath
and is checked by the two black Symplegades.
I opened my heart and breathed deeply!
The golden fleece shivered on the sea.
Hers the colour the shudder and the skin
hers the mountain-ridges on the horizon of my palm.
I opened my heart
full of images that vanished at once, the seed of Proteus.

Here I gazed at the moon
dyed in the blood
of a young she-wolf.

*Spetses, August 1934*

## Sirocco 7 Levante

*For D. I. Antoniou*

Things that changed our shape
deeper than thought and more so
our own like blood and more so
sank into the midday heat
behind the masts.

Among chains and commands
no one remembers.

Other days other nights
bodies, pain and pleasure
the bitterness of human nakedness shattered
lower even than the pepper trees along dusty roads
and so many charms and so many symbols
on the final branch;
in the shade of the big ship
memory's a shade.

The hands that touched us don't belong to us, only
deeper, when the roses darken,
a rhythm in the mountain's shadow – crickets –
moistens our silence in the night
seeking the sea's sleep
slipping towards the sea's sleep.

In the shade of the big ship
as the capstan whistled
I abandoned tenderness to the money-changers.

*Pelion, 19 August 1935*

## In the Manner of G. S.

Wherever I travel Greece wounds me.

On Pelion among the chestnut trees the Centaur's shirt
slipped through the leaves to fold around my body
as I climbed the slope and the sea came after me
climbing too like mercury in a thermometer
till we found the mountain waters.
On Santorini touching islands that were sinking
hearing a pipe play somewhere on the pumice-stone
my hand was nailed to the gunwale
by an arrow shot suddenly
from the confines of a vanished youth.
At Mycenae I raised the great stones and the treasures of the
      house of Atreus
and slept with them at the hotel 'Belle Hélène de Ménélas';
they disappeared only at dawn when Cassandra crowed,
a cock hanging from her black throat.
On Spetses, Poros and Mykonos
the barcaroles sickened me.

What do they want, all those who believe
they're in Athens or Piraeus?
Someone comes from Salamis and asks someone else
      whether he 'issues forth from Omonia Square'.
'No, I issue forth from Syntagma,' replies the other,
      pleased;
'I met Yianni and he treated me to an ice cream.'
In the meantime Greece is travelling
and we don't know anything, we don't know we're all
      sailors out of work,

we don't know how bitter the port becomes when all the
     ships have gone;
we mock those who do know.

Strange people! they say they're in Attica but they're really
     nowhere;
they buy sugared almonds to get married
they carry hair tonic, have their photographs taken
the man I saw today sitting against a background of pigeons
     and flowers
let the hands of the old photographer smoothe away the
     wrinkles
left on his face
by all the birds in the sky.

Meanwhile Greece goes on travelling, always travelling
and if we see 'the Aegean flower with corpses'
it will be with those who tried to catch the big ship by
     swimming after it
those who got tired of waiting for the ships that cannot
     move
the ELSI, the SAMOTHRAKI, the AMVRAKIKOS.
The ships hoot now that dusk falls on Piraeus,
hoot and hoot, but no capstan moves,
no chain gleams wet in the vanishing light,
the captain stands like a stone in white and gold.

Wherever I travel Greece wounds me,
curtains of mountains, archipelagos, naked granite.
They call the one ship that sails AG ONIA 937.

                    *M/s* Aulis, *waiting to sail.*
                         ***Summer 1936***

## The Old Man

So many flocks have passed so many poor
and rich riders, some
from distant villages had spent
the night in roadside ditches
lighting fires against the wolves: do you see
the ashes? Blackish circles cicatrized.
He's full of marks like the road.
In the dry well above they'd thrown the rabid
dogs. He's got no eyes, he's full
of marks, he's light; the wind blows;
he distinguishes nothing, knows everything,
empty sheath of a cicada on a hollow tree.
He's got no eyes, not even in his hands, he knows
dawn and dusk, knows the stars,
their blood doesn't nourish him, nor is
he dead, he has no race, he won't die,
they'll simply forget him, he has no ancestors.
His tired fingernails
inscribe crosses on decayed memories
while the wind blows darkly. It snows.

I saw the hoar-frost around the faces
I saw the lips moist, tears frozen
in the corner of the eye, I saw the line
of pain by the nostrils and the effort
at the roots of the hand, I saw the body come to an end.
He isn't alone, this shadow
bound to a dry inflexible stick
he doesn't bend to lie down, he can't:
sleep will have scattered his joints
as playthings into the hands of children.

He commands like dead branches
that break when night comes and the wind
wakes in the ravines
he commands the shades of men
not the man in the shadow
who hears nothing but the low voices
of earth and sea there where they mix
with the voice of destiny. He stands upright
on the bank, among piles of bones
among heaps of yellow leaves:
empty cage that waits
for the hour of fire.

*Drenovo, February 1937*

# MR STRATIS
# THALASSINOS

And he was preparing to cry out
to show that he wasn't dead.

– SOLOMOS, *The Woman of Zakynthos*

# Five Poems by Mr S. Thalassinos

## I HAMPSTEAD

Like a bird with broken wing
that had travelled through wind for years
like a bird unable to endure
tempest and wind
the evening falls.
On the green grass
three thousand angels had danced the day long
naked as steel
the pale evening falls;
the three thousand angels
gathered in their wings, became
a dog
forgotten
that barks
alone
and searches for its master
or the Second Coming
or a bone.
Now I long for a little quiet
all I want is a hut on a hill
or near a sea-shore
all I want in front of my window
is a sheet immersed in bluing
spread there like the sea
all I want in my vase
is even a false carnation
red paper wound on wire
so that the wind
the wind can control it easily

as much as it wants to.
The evening would fall
the flocks would echo descending to their fold
like some quite simple happy thought
and I would lie down to sleep
because I wouldn't have
even a candle to light,
light,
to read.


*1931*

## II   PSYCHOLOGY

This gentleman
takes his bath each morning
in the waters of the Dead Sea
then dons a bitter smile
for business and clients.

### III   ALL THINGS PASS AWAY

We forgot our heroic dispute with the Eumenides
we fell asleep, they thought we were dead and they fled
    shouting
'Yiou! Yiou! Pououou . . . pax!'
cursing the gods that protect us.

## IV   FIRES OF ST JOHN

Our fate: spilled lead; our fate can't change –
nothing's to be done.
They spilled the lead in water under the stars, and may the
  fires burn.

If you stand naked before a mirror at midnight you see,
you see a man moving through the mirror's depths
the man destined to rule your body
in loneliness and silence, the man
of loneliness and silence
and may the fires burn.

At the hour when one day ends and the next has not begun
at the hour when time is suspended
you must find the man who then and now, from the very
  beginning, ruled your body
you must look for him so that someone else at least
will find him, after you are dead.

It is the children who light the fires and cry out before the
  flames in the hot night (Was there ever a fire that some
  child did not light, O Herostratus)
and throw salt on the flames to make them crackle (How
  strangely the houses – crucibles for men – suddenly stare
  at us when the flame's reflection caresses them).

But you who knew the stone's grace on the sea-whipped rock
the evening when stillness fell
heard from far off the human voice of loneliness and silence
inside your body

that night of St John
when all the fires went out
and you studied the ashes under the stars.

## V   NIJINSKY

He appeared as I was staring at the lighted coals in my fireplace. He held in his hands a large box of red matches which he displayed to me like a conjuror taking an egg out of the nose of the person in the next seat. He struck a match, set fire to the box, disappeared behind an enormous flame, and then stood before me. I recall his crimson smile and his vitreous eyes. A hurdy-gurdy in the street went on repeating the same note. I don't know how to describe what he was wearing, but he kept making me think of a purple cypress. Gradually his arms began to separate from his taut body and to form a cross. Where did so many birds come from? It was as if he'd had them hidden under his wings. They flew clumsily, madly, violently, knocking against the walls of the narrow room, against the window-panes, then covered the floor as though wounded. I felt a warm layer of down and pulsations growing at my feet. I gazed at him, a strange fever possessed my body like a current coursing through it. When he'd finished raising his arms and his palms were together, he gave a sudden leap, as if the spring of a watch had broken in front of me. He knocked against the ceiling, making it echo with the sound of a cymbal, extended his right arm, seized the wire of the lamp, moved slightly, relaxed, then began to describe with his body a figure of eight against the darkness. The sight made me dizzy and I covered my face with both hands, crushing the darkness against my eyelids, while the hurdy-gurdy went on repeating the same note and then stopped abruptly. A sudden icy wind struck me; I felt my legs go numb. Now I also heard the low velvety sound of a flute, followed immediately by a heavy and regular beating. I opened my eyes and again saw him, standing tiptoe on a crystal sphere in the middle of the room, in his mouth a strange green flute over which he was running his fingers as though there were thousands of them. The birds now came back to life in an extraordinary order, rose up, mingled, formed into a cortège as wide as my outspread arms, and went out into the night through the window that was somehow open. When the last flutter had died away and only a suffocating smell of hunting was left, I decided to look him in the face. There was no face: above the purple body, seemingly headless, he sported a golden mask, of the kind found in Mycenaean tombs, with a pointed beard reaching down to the throat. I tried to get up, but I'd hardly made the first movement when a cataclysmic sound, like a pile of kettledrums collapsing in a funeral march, rooted me to the spot. It was the mask. His face appeared again as I'd originally seen it – the eyes, the smile, and something which I now remarked for the first time: the white skin suspended from two black curls that pinned it into place at the temples. He tried to leap but no longer possessed his initial agility. I think he even stumbled against a book fallen there by accident, and he knelt down on one knee. Now I could observe him carefully. I saw the pores of his skin oozing fine beads of sweat. Something like breathlessness came over me. I tried to discover why his eyes had seemed so strange. He closed them and began to get up; but it must have been terribly difficult, for he seemed to concentrate all his strength without being able to do anything. He even knelt now on the other knee as well. The white skin seemed terribly pale, like yellow ivory, and his black hair was lifeless. Though I was witnessing an agonizing struggle, I had the feeling that I was better, that I'd triumphed over something.

Before I could draw breath I saw him, fallen full length now, plunge into a green pagoda portrayed on my carpet.

# Mr Stratis Thalassinos Describes a Man

1

But what's wrong with that man?
All afternoon (yesterday the day before yesterday and
    today) he's been sitting there staring at a flame
he bumped into me at evening as he went downstairs
he said to me:
'The body dies the water clouds the soul
hesitates
and the wind forgets always forgets
but the flame doesn't change.'
He also said to me:
'You know I love a woman who's gone away perhaps to the
    nether world; that's not why I seem so deserted
I try to keep myself going with a flame
because it doesn't change.'
Then he told me the story of his life.

## 2    CHILD

When I began to grow up the trees tormented me –
why do you smile? Were you thinking of spring, so harsh
    for children?
I was very fond of the green leaves
I think I learned a little at school simply because the
    blotting-paper on my desk was also green.
It was the roots of the trees that tormented me when in the
    warmth of winter they'd come and wind themselves
    around my body.
I had no other dreams as a child.
That's how I got to know my body.

3   ADOLESCENT

In the summer of my sixteenth year a strange voice sang in
     my ears;
it was, I remember, at the sea's edge, among the red nets
     and a boat abandoned on the sand, a skeleton
I tried to get closer to that voice by laying my ear to the sand
the voice disappeared
but there was a shooting star
as though I were seeing a shooting star for the first time
and on my lips the salt taste of waves.
From that night the roots of the trees no longer came to me.
The next day a journey opened in my mind and closed
     again, like a picture-book;
I thought of going down to the shore every evening
first to learn about the shore and then to go to sea;
the third day I fell in love with a girl on a hill;
she had a small white cottage like a country chapel
an old mother at the window, glasses bent low over her
     knitting, always silent
a pot of basil a pot of carnations –
I think she was called Vasso, Frosso, or Billio;
so I forgot the sea.
One Monday in October
I found a broken pitcher in front of the white cottage
Vasso (for short) appeared in a black dress, her hair
     uncombed, her eyes red.
When I questioned her she said:
'She died, the doctor said she died because we didn't kill the
     black cock when we dug the foundations . . . Where
     could we find a black cock around here . . . ? Only white
     flocks . . . and in the market the chickens are sold
     already plucked.'

I hadn't imagined grief and death would be like that;
I left and went back to sea.
That night, on the deck of the *St Nicholas*, I dreamt of a very
   old olive tree weeping.

4   YOUNG MAN

I sailed for a year with Captain Odysseus
I was fine
in fair weather I made myself comfortable in the prow
        beside the mermaid
I sang of her red lips as I gazed at the flying fish,
in storms I took refuge in a corner of the hold with the
        ship's dog who kept me warm.
One morning at the end of the year I saw minarets
the mate told me:
'That's Saint Sophia, tonight I'll take you to the women.'
So I got to know those women who wear only stockings –
those we select, in fact.
It was a strange place
a garden with two walnut trees a trellis a well
a wall surrounding it with broken glass along the top
a gutter singing: 'On the stream of my life . . . '.
Then for the first time I saw a heart
pierced by the familiar arrow
drawn in charcoal on the wall.
I saw the leaves of the vine yellow
fallen to the ground
stuck to the flagstones to the humble mud
and I started to go back to the ship.
Then the mate seized me by the collar and threw me into the
        well:
warm water and so much life around the skin . . .
Afterwards the girl, playing idly with her right breast, told
        me:
'I'm from Rhodes, at thirteen they got me engaged for a
        hundred paras.'
And the gutter sang: 'On the stream of my life . . . '.

I recalled the broken pitcher in the cool afternoon and I
    thought:
'She'll die too, how will she die?'
All I said to her was:
'Careful, you'll ruin it, it's your livelihood.'
That evening on the ship I couldn't bear to go near the
    mermaid, I was ashamed of facing her.

## 5   MAN

Since then I've seen many new landscapes: green plains intermingling soil and sky, man and seed, in an irresistible dampness; plane trees and fir trees; lakes with wrinkled visions and swans immortal because they'd lost their voices – scenery unfolded by my willing companion, that strolling player, as he sounded the long horn that had ruined his lips and that destroyed with its shrill note whatever I managed to build, like the trumpet at Jericho. I saw an old picture in some low-ceilinged room; a lot of people were admiring it. It showed the raising of Lazarus. I don't recall either the Christ in it or the Lazarus. Only, in one corner, the disgust portrayed on someone's face as he gazed at the miracle as if he were smelling it. He was trying to protect his breathing with the huge cloth draped around his head. This 'Renaissance' gentleman taught me not to expect too much from the Second Coming...

They told us you'll conquer when you submit.
We submitted and found ashes.
They told us you'll conquer when you love.
We loved and found ashes.
They told us you'll conquer when you abandon your life.
We abandoned our life and found ashes.

We found ashes. What remains is to rediscover our life, now that we've nothing left. I imagine that he who'll rediscover life, in spite of so much paper, so many emotions, so many debates and so much teaching, will be someone like us, only with a slightly tougher memory. We ourselves can't help still remembering what we're given. He'll remember only what he's gained from each of his offerings. What can a flame remember? If it remembers a little less than is necessary, it goes out; if it remembers a little more than is necessary, it goes out. If only it could teach us, while it burns, to remember correctly. I've come to an end: if only someone else could begin at the point where I've ended. There are times when I have the impression that I've reached the limit, that everything's in its place, ready to sing together in harmony. The machine on the point of starting. I can even imagine it in motion, alive, like something unsuspectedly new. But there's still something: an infinitesimal obstacle, a grain of sand, shrinking and shrinking yet unable to disappear completely. I don't know what I ought to say or what I ought to do. Sometimes that obstacle seems to me like a tear-drop wedged into some articulation of the orchestra, keeping it silent until it's been dissolved. And I have an unbearable feeling that all the rest of my life won't be sufficient to dissolve this drop within my soul. And I'm haunted by the thought that, if they were to burn me alive, this obstinate moment would be the last to surrender.

Who will help us? Once, when I was still a seaman, one July afternoon, I found myself alone on some island, crippled in the sun. A fair Etesian wind brought tender thoughts to my mind; and it was then that a young woman, her transparent dress showing the lines of her body, slender and positive like a gazelle's, and a man, silent as he gazed into her eyes across the few feet that separated them, came and sat down not far from where I was. They spoke in a language I didn't understand. She called him Jim. But their words had no weight and their glances, mingled and motionless, left their eyes blind. I always think of them because they're the only people I've ever seen who didn't have the grasping or hunted look that I've seen in everyone else. That look that classes them either with a pack of wolves or a flock of sheep. I met them again the same day in one of those island chapels one stumbles upon only to lose again as soon as one gets out. They were still keeping the same distance from each other; but then they came together and kissed. The woman became a cloudy image and vanished, small as she was. I wondered whether they knew how they'd escaped from the world's nets . . .

It's time for me to go. I know a pine tree that overhangs the sea. At noon it provides the tired body with a shade as measured as our life, and at evening the wind passing through its needles strikes up a strange song, like souls that have abolished death the moment they again start becoming skin and lips. Once I spent the night awake under that tree. At daybreak I was as fresh as if they'd just cut me out of the quarry.

Ah, if one could at least live like that, not at odds with things.

*London, 5 June 1932*

# Notes for a 'Week'

*British-grown daffodils*

## MONDAY

Among the bending asphodels the blind are sleeping
a crowd of blind people and the asphodels bend
blackened by the hoar-frost of dawn.
(I remember the paphiopedila of another winter
enclosed in the hothouse heat.
Enough of life.)
Their pillows, demolished instruments
rickety phonographs
harmonicas full of holes
organs fallen to their knees;
are they dead?
You can't make out a motionless blind man easily.
Sometimes their dreams come alive, that's why I say they're
     sleeping.
All around on the houses, marble robes of angels beckon me
the river doesn't roll, it has forgotten the sea
and yet there is the sea and who will drain it dry?
The blind are sleeping,
angels run naked in their veins
they drink their blood and they make them prudent
and the heart with its terrible eyes calculates
when it will run dry.
I look at the river
sudden light puffs of wind pass under the impotent sun
nothing else, the river waits;
pity those who wait.
Nothing else; that's enough for today.

## TUESDAY

*'I went down to St James Infirmary.'*

I got lost in the town.
The gardens are hidden by the hospital of Don Juan Tavera.
Streets winding round advertisements.
Each man walks without knowing
whether he's at a beginning or an end,
whether he's going to his mother, his daughter, or his
    mistress
whether he'll judge or be judged
whether he'll escape, whether he's escaped already;
he doesn't know.
At every corner a gramophone shop
in every shop a hundred gramophones
for each gramophone a hundred records
on every record
someone living plays with someone dead.
Take the steel needle and separate them
if you can.
Now which poet? Do you remember which poet
tried out the steel needle
on the seams of the human skull?

Do you remember his song that night?
I remember that he asked us for an aspirin
his eyes moved inside black rings
he was pale and two deep wrinkles
bound his forehead. Or was it you
maybe? Or me? Or was it maybe
silent Antigone with those shoulders
rounded over her breasts?
I kept her with me ten nights
and each dawn she would weep for her child.

I remember I was looking for a pharmacy.
They were all closed. Who for, I don't know.

I got lost in the town
no one is going to remove the hospital
full of crippled children gesturing
at me or at others following me.
Odours of medicine in the air
turn heavy, fall in love and mesh
with vapours from cars going off
to the country with Pre-Raphaelite couples
thoroughly blond if somehow a bit evaporated.

In the spring of 1923, Livia Rimini,
the film star, died in her bath;
they found her dead, perfume all around,
and the water not yet cold.
Yet in the movies yesterday
she gazed at me with her useless eyes.

WEDNESDAY

*ad vigilias albas*

– Why doesn't it get dark?
– Have a look if you want to, the new moon must have
    come out somewhere.
– Everybody looks at what you're going to do
and you look at the crowds looking at you;
the glances inscribe a tight circle
that can't be broken.
If someone is born the circle will widen
if someone dies the circle will shrink
yet so little, and for so short a time.
And the four other senses follow the same geometry.
If we were to love, the circle would break,
we'd close our eyelashes a second.
But we can't love.

They were lovely, your eyes, but you didn't know where
    to look
and when you said we ought to go because it was dark,
you turned and looked me in the eyes and a bat
flew off, inscribing triangles . . .
The gramophone started up again.
Our bats now inscribe
circles that shrink as they fly
from one man to another man and on to another
no one escapes
and life is rich because we're many
and all of us the same
and life is rich because we come up with perfected devices
when the senses decline.
Brothers, we've shared our bread and our pain.
No one hungers any longer, no one suffers

and all of us have the same stature. Look at us!
We look at you. We too. We too. We too.
There is nothing beyond.
– But the sea:
I don't know that they've drained it dry.

## THURSDAY

I saw her die many times
sometimes crying in my arms
sometimes in a stranger's arms
sometimes alone, naked;
this is the way she lived with me.
Now at last I know there's nothing further
and I wait.
If I'm sorry, it's a private matter
like the feeling for things so simple
that, as they say, one's passed beyond them;
and yet I'm sorry still because
I too didn't become (as I would have wished)
like the grass I heard sprouting
one night near a pine tree;
because I didn't follow the sea
another night when the waters were withdrawing
gently drinking their own bitterness,
and I didn't even understand, as I groped in the damp
      seaweed,
how much honour remains in the hands of men.
All this passed by slowly and conclusively
like the barges with faded names:
Helen of Sparta, Tyrannus, Gloria Mundi
they passed under the bridges beyond the chimneys
with two stooping men at the prow and stern
naked to the waist;
they passed, I can't distinguish anything, in the morning fog
the sheep, curled, ruminating, barely stand out
nor does the moon stand out above
the waiting river;
only seven lances plunged in the water
stagnant, bloodless

and sometimes on the flagstones, sadly lit
under the squint-eyed castle,
drawn with red and yellow pencil:
the Nazarene, showing his wound.
'Don't throw your heart to the dogs.
Don't throw your heart to the dogs.'
Her voice sinks as the clock strikes;
your will, I sought your will.

FRIDAY

Since then how many times has there passed before me a woman with only her hair, eyes and breasts left, nothing else – mermaid travelling the seas – and with the fresh air circulating between them like blue blood.

SATURDAY

– 'I haven't forgotten anything,
everything's in its place, arranged in order, waiting for the
      hand to choose;
only I couldn't find the childhood years
nor the place where the hero of the drama was born
nor the first impressions
those he recalls in the fifth act
at the height of the disaster.
All the rest, there it is, in order:
the masks for the three main emotions
and for the intermediary ones
the pleated costumes ready to move,
the curtains, the lights,
Medea's slaughtered children,
the poison and the knife.
In that box there's life when it starts getting unbearable:
if you put your ear close you'll hear it breathing;
make sure you don't open it before the Furies whistle.
In that glass you'll find love of the body
and in that other glass – the blue one – love of the soul:
make sure you don't confuse them.
And in that drawer is Nessus's shirt
(Act Five, Scene Three);
you remember the speech that begins:
'Enough of life! Io! Io!'
Here's the trumpet that destroys the palace
revealing the queen in her iniquity;
that's the microphone switch –
they'll hear you at the far end of the world.
Let's go. Lights! Good luck!'

– 'Just a moment, who am I going to play? Who will I kill?
And these people looking at me –
what will make them believe that justice protects me?
What will make them believe it?
O could we only love
like bees at least
not like pigeons
like shells at least
not like sirens
like ants at least
not like plane trees . . .
But don't you see them, they're all blind!
The blind are sleeping . . . '

– 'Wonderful. You can continue.'

## SUNDAY

Two heavy horses and a slow carriage, that or something
     else,
in the street outside my window:
that's the noise.
Soon it'll be dark; I see a pediment of amputated statues still
     looking at me.
What do statues weigh?
I prefer a drop of blood to a glass of ink.


*Summer, 1933*

# SKETCHES
# FOR A SUMMER

# A Word for Summer

We've returned to autumn again; summer,
like an exercise book we're tired of writing in, remains
full of deletions, abstract designs,
question marks in the margin; we've returned
to the season of eyes gazing
into the mirror under the electric light
closed lips and people strangers
in rooms in streets under the pepper trees
while the headlights of cars massacre
thousands of pale masks.
We've returned; we always set out to return
to solitude, a fistful of earth, to the empty hands.

And yet I used to love Syngrou Avenue
the double rise and fall of the great road
bringing us out miraculously to the sea
the eternal sea, to cleanse us of our sins;
I used to love certain unknown people
met suddenly at the end of day
talking to themselves like captains of a sunken armada,
evidence that the world is large.
And yet I used to love these roads here, these columns,
even though I was born on the other shore, close
to reeds and rushes, islands
where water gushed from the sand to quench
the thirst of a rower, even though I was born
close to the sea that I unwind and wind on my fingers
when I'm tired – I no longer know where I was born.

There still remains the yellow essence, summer,
and your hands touching medusas on the water

your eyes suddenly open, the first
eyes of the world, and the sea caves:
feet naked on the red soil.
There still remains the blond marble youth, summer,
a little salt dried in the rock's hollow
a few pine needles after the rain
scattered and red like broken nets.

I don't understand these faces I don't understand them,
sometimes they imitate death and then again
they gleam with the low life of a glow-worm
with a limited effort, hopeless,
squeezed between two wrinkles,
between two stained café tables;
they kill one another, grow smaller,
stick like postage stamps to window-panes –
the faces of the other tribe.

We walked together, shared bread and sleep
tasted the same bitterness of parting
built our houses with what stones we had
set out in ships, knew exile, returned
found our women waiting –
they scarcely knew us, no one knows us.
And the companions wore statues, wore the naked
empty chairs of autumn, and the companions
destroyed their own faces: I don't understand them.
There still remains the yellow desert, summer,
waves of sand receding to the final circle
a drum's beat, merciless, endless,
flaming eyes sinking into the sun
hands in the manner of birds cutting the sky
saluting ranks of the dead who stand at attention

hands lost at a point beyond my control and mastering me:
your hands touching the free wave.

*Autumn, 1936*

## Epiphany, 1937

The flowering sea and the mountains in the moon's waning
the great stone close to the Barbary figs and the asphodels
the jar that refused to go dry at the end of day
and the closed bed by the cypress trees and your hair
golden; the stars of the Swan and that other star, Aldebaran.

I've kept a rein on my life, kept a rein on my life, travelling
among yellow trees in driving rain
on silent slopes loaded with beech leaves,
no fire on their peaks; it's getting dark.
I've kept a rein on my life; on your left hand a line
a scar at your knee, perhaps they exist
on the sand of the past summer perhaps
they remain there where the north wind blew as I hear
an alien voice around the frozen lake.
The faces I see do not ask questions nor does the woman
bent as she walks giving her child the breast.
I climb the mountains; dark ravines; the snow-covered
plain, into the distance stretches the snow-covered plain,
        they ask nothing
neither time shut up in dumb chapels nor
hands outstretched to beg, nor the roads.
I've kept a rein on my life whispering in a boundless
        silence
I no longer know how to speak nor how to think; whispers
like the breathing of the cypress tree that night
like the human voice of the night sea on pebbles
like the memory of your voice saying 'happiness'.

I close my eyes looking for the secret meeting-place of the
        waters
under the ice the sea's smile, the closed wells
groping with my veins for those veins that escape me
there where the water-lilies end and that man
who walks blindly across the snows of silence.
I've kept a rein on my life, with him, looking for the water
        that touches you
heavy drops on green leaves, on your face
in the empty garden, drops in the motionless reservoir
striking a swan dead in its white wings
living trees and your eyes riveted.

This road has no end, has no relief, however hard you try
to recall your childhood years, those who left, those
lost in sleep, in the graves of the sea,
however much you ask bodies you've loved to stoop
under the harsh branches of the plane trees there
where a ray of the sun, naked, stood still
and a dog leapt and your heart shuddered,
the road has no relief; I've kept a rein on my life.

                        The snow
and the water frozen in the hoofmarks of the horses.

## Raven

*In memoriam E. A. P.*

Years like wings. What does the motionless raven
    remember?
What do the dead close to the roots of trees remember?
Your hands had the colour of an apple ready to fall,
and that voice which always returns, that low voice.

Those who travel watch the sail and the stars
they hear the wind they hear the other sea beyond the wind
near them like a closed shell, they don't hear
anything else, don't look among the cypress shadows
for a lost face, a coin, don't ask,
seeing a raven on a dry branch, what it remembers.
It remains motionless just over my hours
like the soul of an eyeless statue;
there's a whole crowd gathered in that bird
thousands of people forgotten, wrinkles obliterated
broken embraces and uncompleted laughter,
arrested works, silent stations
a deep sleep of golden spangles.
It remains motionless. It gazes at my hours. What does it
    remember?
There are many wounds inside those invisible people
    within it
suspended passions waiting for the Second Coming
humble desires cleaving to the ground
children slaughtered and women exhausted at daybreak.
Does it weigh the dry branch down? Does it weigh down
the roots of the yellow tree, the shoulders
of other men, strange figures

sunk in the ground, not daring to touch even a drop of
    water?
Does it weigh down anywhere?
Your hands had a weight like hands in water
in the sea caves, a light careless weight
pushing the sea away to the horizon to the islands
with that movement we make sometimes when we dismiss
    an ugly thought.
The plain is heavy after the rain; what does the black
static flame against the grey sky remember
wedged between man and the memory of man
between the wound and the hand that inflicted the wound a
    black lance,
the plain darkened drinking the rain, the wind dropped
my own impetus can't shift it, who will shift it?
Within memory, a gulf – a startled breast
between the shadows struggling to become man and
    woman again
stagnant life between sleep and death.

Your hands always moved towards the sea's slumber
caressing the dream that gently ascended the golden
    spider-web
bearing into the sun the host of constellations
the closed eyelids the closed wings . . .

*Koritsa, winter 1937*

Flowers of the rock facing the green sea
with veins that reminded me of other loves
glowing in the slow fine rain,
flowers of the rock, figures
that came when no one spoke and spoke to me
that let me touch them after the silence
among pine trees, oleanders and plane trees.

The warm water reminds me each morning
that I have nothing else alive near me.

## Epitaph

Coals in the fog
were roses rooted in your heart
and the ashes covered your face
each morning.

Plucking cypress shadows
you left a summer ago.

Between two bitter moments you don't have time even to
     breathe
between your face and your face
the tender form of a child takes shape and vanishes.

In the sea caves
there's a thirst there's a love
there's an ecstasy
all hard like shells
you can hold them in your palm.

In the sea caves
for whole days I gazed into your eyes
and I didn't know you nor did you know me.

Stop looking for the sea and the waves' fleece pushing the
    caïques along
under the sky we are the fish and the trees are the seaweed.

# Logbook I

We remain in this position awaiting orders.

– FROM *Logbooks*

Meanwhile it sometimes seems better to me
to sleep than to be so completely without companions as we
    are,
to be always waiting like this; and what's to be done or said in the
    meanwhile
I don't know, and what is the use of poets in a mean-spirited
    time?

– FRIEDRICH HÖLDERLIN, 'Bread and Wine'

## Mathios Paskalis Among the Roses

I've been smoking steadily all morning
if I stop the roses will embrace me
they'll choke me with thorns and fallen petals
they grow crookedly, each with the same rose colour
they gaze, expecting to see someone go by; no one goes by.
Behind the smoke of my pipe I watch them
scentless on their weary stems.
In the other life a woman said to me: 'You can touch this
    hand,
and this rose is yours, it's yours, you can take it
now or later, whenever you like.'

I go down the steps smoking still,
and the roses follow me down excited
and in their manner there's something of that voice
at the root of a cry, there where one starts shouting
'mother' or 'help'
or the small white cries of love.

It's a small garden full of roses
a few square yards descending with me
as I go down the steps, without the sky;
and her aunt would say to her: 'Antigone, you forgot your
    exercises today,
at your age I never wore corsets, not in my time.'
Her aunt was a pitiful creature: veins in relief,
wrinkles all around her ears, a nose ready to die;
but her words were always full of prudence.
One day I saw her touching Antigone's breast
like a small child stealing an apple.

♦

Is it possible that I'll meet the old woman now as I go down?
She said to me as I left: 'Who knows when we'll meet
    again?'
And then I read of her death in old newspapers
of Antigone's marriage and the marriage of Antigone's
    daughter
without the steps coming to an end or my tobacco
which leaves on my lips the taste of a haunted ship
with a mermaid crucified to the wheel while she was still
    beautiful.

*Koritsa, summer '37*

# Fine Autumn Morning

*For Mrs Dononko*

There, you see, at last I love these mountains with this light
their skin wrinkled like an elephant's belly
when his eyes shrink with age.
There, you see, I love these poplars, few as they are,
raising their shoulders into the sun.
The tall Ghegs and the short Tosks
summer with the sickle and winter with the axe
the same things again and again, the same movements
in the same bodies: the monotony is broken.
What's the Muezzin saying from the top of his minaret?
    Listen!
He's leaned over to embrace a blonde doll on a nearby
    balcony.
She waves two pink little hands at the sky
refusing to be ravished.
But the minaret and the balcony lean like the tower of Pisa
    you hear only whispers, it isn't the leaves or the water
'Allah! Allah!' it isn't even the breeze, a strange prayer.
A cock crowed, he must be blond –
O soul in love that has soared to the heights!

There, you see, at last I love these mountains hunched up
    like this,
the ancient flock about me with these wrinkles.
Has anyone thought of telling a mountain's fortune as you
    read the palm of a hand?

Has anyone thought of it? . . . O that insistent thought
shut up in an empty box, wilfully
beating the cardboard without a pause all night long
like a mouse gnawing the floor.
The monotony is broken, O you who've soared to the
        heights, there, you see, I love
even that buffalo on the Macedonian plain, so patient,
so unhurried, as if knowing that no one gets anywhere,
recalling the arrogant head of the warlike Vercingetorix
*Tel qu'en lui-même enfin l'éternité le change.*

                                        *Koritsa, 1937*

# Piazza San Niccolò

*Longtemps je me suis couché de bonne heure*
                    the house
full of grilles and distrust when you examine it closely in its
    dark corners –
'For years I used to go to bed early,' it whispers
'I would gaze at the picture of Hylas and the picture of Mary
    Magdalene
before saying goodnight. I would gaze at the white light of
    the candelabra
the glistening metal, and it would be difficult for me to leave
the last voices of day.'
The house, when you examine its old cornices closely,
wakens with a mother's footsteps on the stairs
the hand that arranges the covers or fixes the mosquito-net
the lips that put out the candle's flame.

And all this is an old story that no longer interests anyone;
we've hardened our hearts and grown up.
The mountain's coolness never descends lower than the
    bell-tower
that counts out the hours in monologue, as we observe
when into the courtyard of an afternoon
comes aunt Daria Dimietrovna née Trofimovitch.
The mountain's coolness never touches the steady hand of
    St Nicholas
nor the druggist who looks out between a red and black
    sphere
like a petrified transatlantic liner.

To find the mountain's coolness you must climb higher than
    the bell-tower
and the hand of St Nicholas
about 70 or 80 metres higher, nothing really.
Yet there you whisper as you would when going to bed
    early
and in the ease of sleep the bitterness of separation would
    disappear
not many words, one or two only and that's enough
since the water rolls on and they're not afraid it will stop
you whisper resting your head on a friend's shoulder
as though you hadn't grown up in the silent house
with faces that became heavy and made us awkward
    strangers.
Yet there, a little higher than the bell-tower, your life
    changes.
It's no great matter to climb up but it's very difficult for you
    to change
when the house is in the stone church and your heart in the
    darkening house
and all the doors locked by the huge hand of St Nicholas.

*Pelion–Koritsa, summer–autumn '37*

# Our Sun

This sun was mine and yours; we shared it.
Who's suffering behind the golden silk, who's dying?
A woman beating her dry breasts cried out: 'Cowards,
they've taken my children and torn them to shreds, you've
    killed them
gazing at the fire-flies at dusk with a strange look,
lost in blind thought.'
The blood was drying on a hand that a tree made green,
a warrior was asleep clutching the lance that cast light
    against his side.

It was ours, this sun, we saw nothing behind the gold
    embroidery
then the messengers came, dirty and breathless,
stuttering unintelligible words
twenty days and nights on the barren earth with thorns only
twenty days and nights feeling the bellies of the horses
    bleeding
and not a moment's break to drink the rain-water.
You told them to rest first and then to speak, the light had
    dazzled you.
They died saying 'We don't have time', touching some rays
    of the sun.
You'd forgotten that no one rests.

A woman howled 'Cowards', like a dog in the night.
Once she would have been beautiful like you
with wet mouth, veins alive beneath the skin,
with love.

This sun was ours; you kept all of it, you wouldn't follow
    me.
And it was then I found out about those things behind the
    gold and the silk:
we don't have time. The messengers were right.

# The Return of the Exile

'My old friend, what are you looking for?
After years abroad you've come back
with images you've nourished
under foreign skies
far from your own country.'

'I'm looking for my old garden;
the trees come to my waist
and the hills resemble terraces
yet as a child
I used to play on the grass
under great shadows
and I would run for hours
breathless over the slopes.'

'My old friend, rest,
you'll get used to it little by little;
together we will climb
the paths you once knew,
we will sit together
under the plane trees' dome.
They'll come back to you little by little,
your garden and your slopes.'

'I'm looking for my old house,
the tall windows
darkened by ivy;
I'm looking for the ancient column
known to sailors.
How can I get into this coop?
The roof comes to my shoulders

and however far I look
I see men on their knees
as though saying their prayers.'

'My old friend, don't you hear me?
You'll get used to it little by little.
Your house is the one you see
and soon friends and relatives
will come knocking at the door
to welcome you back tenderly.'

'Why is your voice so distant?
Raise your head a little
so that I understand you.
As you speak you grow
gradually smaller as though
you're sinking into the ground.'

'My old friend, stop a moment and think:
you'll get used to it little by little.
Your nostalgia has created
a non-existent country, with laws
alien to earth and man.'

'Now I can't hear a sound.
My last friend has sunk.
Strange how from time to time
they level everything down.
Here a thousand scythe-bearing chariots go past
and mow everything down.'

*Athens, spring '38*

# The Container of the Uncontainable

*Good Friday*

Bells like coins falling sound today all over the city
between each peal a new space opens
like a drop of water on the earth: the moment has come,
    raise me up.

## Interlude of Joy

That whole morning we were full of joy,
my God, how full of joy.
First, stones leaves and flowers shone
then the sun
a huge sun all thorns and so high in the sky.
A nymph collected our cares and hung them on the trees
a forest of Judas trees.
Young cupids and satyrs played there and sang
and you could see rose-coloured limbs among the black
    laurels
flesh of little children.
The whole morning long we were full of joy;
the abyss a closed well
tapped by the tender hoof of a young faun.
Do you remember its laugh – how full of joy!
Then clouds rain and the wet earth,
you stopped laughing when you lay down in the hut
and opened your large eyes as you watched
the archangel practising with a fiery sword –
'Inexplicable,' you said, 'inexplicable.
I don't understand people:
no matter how much they play with colours
they all remain pitch-black.'

*Penteli, spring*

## The Leaf of the Poplar

It trembled so, the wind carried it away,
it trembled so, how could the wind not carry it away
in the distance
a sea
in the distance
an island in the sun
and hands grasping the oars
dying the moment the port came into sight
and eyes closed
in sea anemones.

It trembled so much
I wanted it so much
in the cistern with the eucalyptus trees
spring and autumn
in all the woods naked
my God I wanted it.

## Solidarity

It's there, I can't change
with two large eyes behind the wave
on the side where the wind blows
following the wings of birds
it's there with two large eyes
has anyone ever changed himself?

What are you looking for? Your messages
reach the ship altered
your love becomes hatred
your peace becomes tumult
and I can't turn back
to see your faces on the shore.

The large eyes are there
both when I keep fixed on my course
and when the stars fall on the horizon
they are there tethered to space
like a fate more mine than my own.

Your words, a habit of hearing,
hum in the rigging and are lost
do I still believe in your existence
doomed companions, unsubstantial shades?

◆

This world has lost its colour
like last year's seaweed on the beach
dry, grey, at the wind's mercy.

A huge sea two eyes
swift and motionless like the wind
and my sails as long as they last, and my god.

## The Last Day

The day was cloudy. No one could come to a decision;
a light wind was blowing. 'Not a north-easter, the sirocco,'
    someone said.
A few slender cypresses nailed to the slope, and, beyond,
    the sea
grey with shining pools.
The soldiers presented arms as it began to drizzle.
'Not a north-easter, the sirocco,' was the only decision
    heard.
And yet we knew that by the following dawn
nothing would be left to us, neither the woman drinking
    sleep at our side
nor the memory that we were once men,
nothing at all by the following dawn.

'This wind reminds me of spring,' said my friend
as she walked beside me gazing into the distance, 'the spring
that came suddenly in winter by the closed-in sea.
So unexpected. So many years have gone. How are we
    going to die?'

A funeral march meandered through the thin rain.

How does a man die? Strange no one's thought about it.
And for those who thought about it, it was like a
    recollection from old chronicles
from the time of the Crusades or the battle of Salamis.
Yet death is something that happens: how does a man die?
Yet each of us earns his death, his own death, which belongs
    to no one else
and this game is life.

The light was fading from the clouded day, no one decided
    anything.
The following dawn nothing would be left to us,
    everything surrendered, even our hands,
and our women slaves at the springheads and our children in
    the quarries.
My friend, walking beside me, was singing a disjointed
    song:
'In spring, in summer, slaves . . . '
One recalled old teachers who'd left us orphans.
A couple passed, talking:
'I'm sick of the dusk, let's go home,
let's go home and turn on the light.'

*Athens, Feb. '39*

## Spring A. D.

Again with spring
she wore light colours
and with gentle steps
again with spring
again in summer
she was smiling.

Among fresh blossoms
breast naked to the veins
beyond the dry night
beyond the white old men
debating quietly
whether it would be better
to give up the keys
or to pull the rope
and hang from the noose
to leave empty bodies
there where souls couldn't endure
there where the mind couldn't catch up
and knees buckled.

With the new blossoms
the old men failed
and gave up everything
grandchildren and great-grandchildren
the broad fields
the green mountains
love and life
compassion and shelter
rivers and sea;

and they departed like statues
leaving behind a silence
that no sword could cut
that no gallop could break
nor the voices of the young;
and the great loneliness came
the great privation
along with this spring
and settled and spread
like the frost of dawn
caught hold of the high branches
slid down the trunks of trees
and wrapped around our soul.

But she smiled
wearing light colours
like a blossoming almond tree
in yellow flames
and walked along lightly
opening windows
in the delighted sky
without us the luckless ones.
And I saw her breast naked
the waist and the knee,
as the inviolate martyr
inviolate and pure
issues from the torment
to go to heaven,
beyond the inexplicable
whispering of people
in the boundless circus
beyond the black grimace
the sweaty neck

of the exasperated executioner
striking vainly.

The loneliness now a lake
the privation now a lake
untouched and untraceable.

*16 March '39*

# The Jasmine

Whether it's dusk
or dawn's first light
the jasmine stays
always white.

## Narration

That man walks along weeping
no one can say why
sometimes they think he's weeping for lost loves
like those that torture us so much
on summer beaches with the gramophones.

Other people go about their business
endless paper, children growing up, women
ageing awkwardly.
He has two eyes like poppies
like cut spring poppies
and two trickles in the corners of his eyes.

He walks along the streets, never lies down
striding small squares on the earth's back
instrument of a boundless pain
that's finally lost all significance.

Some have heard him speak
to himself as he passed by
about mirrors broken years ago
about broken forms in the mirrors
that no one can ever put together again.
Others have heard him talk about sleep
images of horror on the threshold of sleep
faces unbearable in their tenderness.

We've grown used to him, he's presentable and quiet
only that he walks along weeping continually

like willows on a river-bank you see from the train
as you wake uncomfortably some clouded dawn.

We've grown used to him; like everything else you're used to
he doesn't stand for anything
and I talk to you about him because I can't find
anything that you're not used to;
I pay my respects.

## Morning

Open your eyes and unfold
the black cloth fully and stretch it
open your eyes wide fix your eyes
concentrate concentrate now you know
that the black cloth unfolds
not in sleep nor in water
nor when the eyelids close wrinkled
and sink at an angle like shells
now you know that the black skin of the drum
fully covers your horizon
when you open your eyes rested, like this.
Between the equinox of spring and the equinox of autumn
here the running waters here the garden
here the bees sounding in the branches
and buzzing in a child's ear
and there the sun! and the birds of paradise
a huge sun greater than the light.

# Les Anges Sont Blancs

*To Henry Miller*

> *Tout à coup Louis cessa de frotter ses jambes l'une
> contre l'autre et dit d'une voix lente: 'Les anges
> sont blancs.'*
>
> — BALZAC

Like a sailor in the shrouds he slipped over the tropic of
    Cancer and the tropic of Capricorn
and it was natural he couldn't stand before us at a man's
    height
but looked at us all from the height of a firefly or from the
    height of a pine tree
drawing his breath deeply in the dew of the stars or in the
    dust of the earth.
Naked women with bronze leaves from a Barbary fig tree
    surrounded him
extinguished lamp-posts airing stained bandages of the great
    city
ungainly bodies producing Centaurs and Amazons
when their hair touched the Milky Way.

And days have passed since the first moment he greeted us
    taking his head off and placing it on the iron table
while the shape of Poland changed like ink drunk by
    blotting-paper
and we journeyed among shores of islands bare like strange
    fish-bones on the sand
and the whole sky, empty and white, was a pigeon's huge
    wing beating with a rhythm of silence
and dolphins under the coloured water turned dark quickly
    like the soul's movements

like movements of the imagination and the hands of men
   who grope and kill themselves in sleep
in the huge unbroken rind of sleep that wraps around us,
   common to all of us, our common grave
with brilliant minute crystals crushed by the motion of
   reptiles.
And yet everything was white because the great sleep is
   white and the great death
calm and serene and isolated in an endless silence.
And the cackling of the guinea-hen at dawn and the cock
   that crowed falling into a deep well
and the fire on the mountain-side raising hands of sulphur
   and autumn leaves
and the ship with its forked shoulder-blades more tender
   than the dovetailing of our first love,
all were things isolated even beyond the poem
that you abandoned when you fell heavily along with its last
   word,
knowing nothing any longer among the white eyeballs of
   the blind and the sheets
that you unfold in fever to cover the daily procession
of people who fail to bleed even when they strike
   themselves with axes and nails;
they were things isolated, put somewhere else, and the steps
   of whitewash
descended to the threshold of the past and found silence and
   the door didn't open
and it was as if your friends, in great despair, knocked
   loudly and you were with them
but you heard nothing and dolphins rose around you
   dumbly in the seaweed.
And again you gazed intently and that man, the teethmarks
   of the tropics in his skin,

putting on his dark glasses as if he were going to work with
    a blowlamp,
said humbly, pausing at every word:
'The angels are white flaming white and the eye that would
    confront them shrivels
and there's no other way you've got to become like stone if
    you want their company
and when you look for the miracle you've got to scatter
    your blood to the eight points of the wind
because the miracle is nowhere but circulates in the veins of
    man.'

*Hydra–Athens, Nov. '39*

## The Sentence to Oblivion

> *Who will appraise for us the sentence to oblivion?*
> —G. S.

Stop, passer-by, beside the still lake;
the curly sea and the tormented ships
the roads that wound round mountains and gave birth to stars
all end here on this broad surface.

Now you can watch the swans calmly
look at them: all white like the night's sleep
without touching anywhere they glide on a thin blade
that lifts them barely above the water.

They're like you, stranger, the still wings, and you
    understand them
as the stony eyes of the lions stare at you
and the tree's leaf remains uninscribed in the heavens
and the pen pierced the prison wall.

And yet the birds that slaughtered the village girls were
    none other than these
the blood reddened the milk on the road's flagstones
and their horses cast noiselessly, like molten lead,
illegible shapes into the troughs.

And night suddenly tightened around their arched necks
which didn't sing because there was no way to die
but beat, threshing men's bones blindly.
And their wings cooled the horror.

And what then happened had the same tranquillity as what
    you see before you
the same tranquillity because there wasn't a soul left for us
    to consider
except the power for carving a few signs on the stones
which now have reached the depths below memory.

We too with them, far away, very far away – stop,
    passer-by,
beside the still lake with the immaculate swans
that travel like white tatters through your mind
and waken you to things you lived yet don't remember.

Nor do you remember as you read our characters on the
    stones;
even so you're astonished together with your sheep
that enlarge your body with their wool
now that you feel in your veins a sound of sacrifice.

## The King of Asini

Ἀσίνην τε... – ILIAD

All morning long we looked around the citadel
starting from the shaded side there where the sea
green and without lustre – breast of a slain peacock –
received us like time without an opening in it.
Veins of rock dropped down from high above,
twisted vines, naked, many-branched, coming alive
at the water's touch, while the eye following them
struggled to escape the monotonous see-saw motion,
growing weaker and weaker.

On the sunny side a long empty beach
and the light striking diamonds on the huge walls.
No living thing, the wild doves gone
and the king of Asini, whom we've been trying to find for
    two years now,
unknown, forgotten by all, even by Homer,
only one word in the *Iliad* and that uncertain,
thrown here like the gold burial mask.
You touched it, remember its sound? Hollow in the light
like a dry jar in dug earth:
the same sound that our oars make in the sea.
The king of Asini a void under the mask
everywhere with us everywhere with us, under a name:
'Ἀσίνην τε...Ἀσίνην τε...'
                                and his children statues
and his desires the fluttering of birds, and the wind
in the gaps between his thoughts, and his ships

anchored in a vanished port:
under the mask a void.

Behind the large eyes the curved lips the curls
carved in relief on the gold cover of our existence
a dark spot that you see travelling like a fish
in the dawn calm of the sea:
a void everywhere with us.
And the bird, a wing broken,
that flew away last winter
– tabernacle of life –
and the young woman who left to play
with the dog-teeth of summer
and the soul that sought the lower world gibbering
and the country like a large plane-leaf swept along by the
    torrent of the sun
with the ancient monuments and the contemporary sorrow.

And the poet lingers, looking at the stones, and asks himself
does there really exist
among these ruined lines, edges, points, hollows and curves
does there really exist
here where one meets the path of rain, wind and ruin
does there exist the movement of the face, shape of the
    tenderness
of those who've waned so strangely in our lives,
those who remained the shadow of waves and thoughts
    with the sea's boundlessness
or perhaps no, nothing is left but the weight
the nostalgia for the weight of a living existence
there where we now remain unsubstantial, bending

like the branches of a terrible willow tree heaped in
    unremitting despair
while the yellow current slowly carries down rushes
    uprooted in the mud
image of a form that the sentence to everlasting bitterness
    has turned to stone:
the poet a void.

Shieldbearer, the sun climbed warring,
and from the depths of the cave a startled bat
hit the light as an arrow hits a shield:
''Ασίνην τε... 'Ασίνην τε...'. If only that could be the king
    of Asini
we've been searching for so carefully on this acropolis
sometimes touching with our fingers his touch upon the
    stones.

*Asini, summer '38–Athens, Jan. '40*

# Logbook II

Sometimes it crosses my mind that the things I write here are nothing other than images that prisoners or sailors tattoo on their skin.

– G. S.

# Days of June '41

The new moon came out over Alexandria
with the old moon in her arms
while we were walking towards the Gate of the Sun
in the heart's darkness – three friends.

Who wants to bathe in the waters of Proteus now?
We looked for metamorphosis in our youth
with desires that played like big fish
in seas suddenly shrinking;
we believed in the body's omnipotence.
And now the new moon has come out embracing
the old; and the beautiful island bleeding,
wounded; the calm island – the strong, innocent island.
And the bodies like broken branches,
like roots uprooted.
                    Our thirst
a guard on horseback turned to stone
at the dark Gate of the Sun –
he doesn't know how to ask for anything: he stands guard
exiled somewhere around here
near the tomb of Alexander the Great.

*Crete–Alexandria–South Africa, May–Sept. '41*

## Postscript

But their eyes are all white, without lashes
and their arms thin as reeds.

Lord, not with these people. I've known
the voices of children at dawn
rushing down green slopes
happy as bees, happy as butterflies
with so many colours.
Lord, not with these people, their voices
don't even leave their mouths –
they stay glued to their yellow teeth.

Yours is the sea and the wind
with a star hung in the firmament.
Lord, they don't know that we are
what we are able to be
healing our wounds with herbs
found on the green slopes,
these slopes nearby, not any others;
that we breathe as we are able to breathe
with a little prayer each dawn
that reaches the shore by crossing
the chasms of memory –
Lord, not with these people. Let your will be done in
    another way.

*11 September '41*

# The Figure of Fate

*Fables pictured in our heart*
*Like a silver schooner offered to the icons*
*Of an empty church, July on the island.*
  – G. S.


The figure of fate over a child's birth,
circling of the stars and the wind on a dark night in February,
old women with healing skills climbing the creaking stairs
and the dry branches of the vine naked in the courtyard.

Over a child's crib the figure of fate black-kerchiefed
smile inexplicable and eyelids lowered and breast white as
     milk
and the door opening and the skipper, sea-whipped,
throwing his wet cap onto a black chest.

These faces and these circumstances pursued you
while you unwound the yarn for your nets on the beach
and again while you watched the hollow of waves as you
     sailed on a broad reach;
on all seas, in every gulf
they were with you, and they were the hardship of life, they
     were the joy.

Now I don't know how to read on:
why they bound you in chains, why they pierced you with
     the spear,
why one night in the forest they parted you from the woman
who watched with startled eyes and couldn't speak at all,
why they deprived you of light, the open sea, bread.

How did we fall, my friend, into the pit of fear?
It wasn't your fate, nor was it decreed for me,
we never sold or bought this kind of merchandise;
who is he who commands and murders behind our backs?
Don't ask; three red horses on the threshing-floor
circle on human bones, their eyes blindfolded;
don't ask, just wait: the blood, the blood
will rise some morning like St George the rider
to nail the dragon to earth with his lance.

*1 October '41*

# Kerk Str. Oost, Pretoria, Transvaal

Jacarandas playing castanets and dancing
threw around their feet a violet snow.
The rest's uninteresting, and that
Venusberg of bureaucracy with its twin
towers and its twin gilt clocks
profoundly torpid like a hippopotamus in blue sky.
And cars raced by showing
backs glistening like dolphins.
At the end of the street waiting for us –
strutting idly about its cage –
was the silver pheasant of China,
the Euplocamus Nychthemerus, as they call it.

And to think we set out, the heart full of shot,
saying goodbye
to Onokrotalos the Pelican – he
with the look of a down-trodden prime minister
in the zoological garden of Cairo.

*October '41*

## Stratis Thalassinos Among the Agapanthi

There are no asphodels, violets or hyacinths;
how then can you talk with the dead?
The dead know the language of flowers only;
so they keep silent
they travel and keep silent, endure and keep silent,
past the region of dreams, past the region of dreams.

If I start to sing I'll call out
and if I call out –
the agapanthi order silence
raising the tiny hand of a blue Arabian child
or even the footfalls of a goose in the air.

It's painful and difficult, the living don't meet my need
first because they do not speak, and then
because I have to ask the dead
in order to go forward any further.
There's no other way: the moment I fall asleep
the companions cut the silver strings
and the pouch of the winds empties.
I fill it and it empties, I fill it and it empties;
I wake
like a goldfish swimming
in the lightning's crevices
and the wind and the flood and the human bodies
and the agapanthi nailed like the arrows of fate
to the unquenchable earth
shaken by convulsive nodding,
as if loaded on an ancient cart
jolting down gutted roads, over old cobble-stones,

the agapanthi, asphodels of the negroes:
How can I grasp this religion?

The first thing God made is love
then comes blood
and the thirst for blood
roused by
the body's sperm as by salt.
The first thing God made is the long journey;
that house there is waiting
with its blue smoke
with its aged dog
waiting for the homecoming so that it can die.
But the dead must guide me;
it is the agapanthi that keep them from speaking,
like the depths of the sea or the water in a glass.
And the companions stay on in the palaces of Circe:
my dear Elpenor! My poor, foolish Elpenor!
Or don't you see them?
– 'Oh help us!' –
On the blackened ridge of Psara.

*Transvaal, 14 January '42*

## An Old Man on the River Bank

*To Nani Panayiotopoulo*

And yet we should consider how we go forward.
To feel is not enough, nor to think, nor to move
nor to put your body in danger in front of an old loophole
when scalding oil and molten lead furrow the walls.

And yet we should consider towards what we go forward,
not as our pain would have it, and our hungry children
and the chasm between us and the companions calling from
     the opposite shore;
nor as the bluish light whispers it in an improvised hospital,
the pharmaceutic glimmer on the pillow of the youth
     operated on at noon;
but it should be in some other way, I would say like
the long river that emerges from the great lakes enclosed
     deep in Africa,
that was once a god and then became a road and a
     benefactor, a judge and a delta;
that is never the same, as the ancient wise men taught,
and yet always remains the same body, the same bed, and
     the same Sign,
the same orientation.

I want nothing more than to speak simply, to be granted
     that grace.
Because we've loaded even our song with so much music
     that it's slowly sinking
and we've decorated our art so much that its features have
     been eaten away by gold

and it's time to say our few words because tomorrow our
    soul sets sail.


If pain is human we are not human beings merely to suffer
    pain;
that's why I think so much these days about the great river,
this meaning that moves forward among herbs and
    greenery
and beasts that graze and drink, men who sow and harvest,
great tombs even and small habitations of the dead.
This current that goes its way and that is not so different
    from the blood of men,
from the eyes of men when they look straight ahead
    without fear in their hearts,
without the daily tremor for trivialities or even for
    important things;
when they look straight ahead like the traveller who is used
    to gauging his way by the stars,
not like us, the other day, gazing at the enclosed garden of a
    sleepy Arab house,
behind the lattices the cool garden changing shape, growing
    larger and smaller,
we too changing, as we gazed, the shape of our desire and
    our hearts,
at noon's precipitation, we the patient dough of a world that
    throws us out and kneads us,
caught in the embroidered nets of a life that was as it should
    be and then became dust and sank into the sands
leaving behind it only that vague dizzying sway of a tall
    palm tree.


*Cairo, 20 June '42*

## Stratis Thalassinos on the Dead Sea

*Sometimes one sees in chapels built on legendary sites
the relevant Biblical description quoted in English
and beneath it: 'THIS IS THE PLACE, GENTLEMEN!'*
    – LETTER OF S. T. FROM JERUSALEM

Jerusalem, drifting city,
Jerusalem, city of refugees.

Sometimes you see at noon
a flock of scattered black leaves
sliding across the asphalt road –
Migratory birds are passing under the sun
but you don't raise your head.

Jerusalem, drifting city!

Unknown tongues of Babel
without relation to the grammar,
to the Lives of the Saints or the Book of Psalms,
that they taught you to spell out in autumn
when they tied the fishing boats to the quays;
unknown tongues glued
like burned-out cigarette-butts to decayed lips.

Jerusalem, city of refugees!

But their eyes all speak the same word,
not the word that became man, God forgive us,
not journeys to see new places, but
the dark train of flight where infants
are fed on the dirt and the sins of their parents
and the middle-aged feel the chasm

broaden between the body –
lagging behind like a wounded camel –
and the soul with what they call its inexhaustible courage.
It is also the ships that carry them,
standing upright like embalmed bishops
in the holds, to moor one evening
in the seaweed of the deep, softly.

Jerusalem, drifting city!

> To the River Jordan
> three monks brought
> a small red caïque
> and moored it to the banks.
> Three from Mount Athos
> sailed for three months
> and moored to a branch,
> on the Jordan banks,
> a refugee's offering.
> They hungered three months
> they thirsted three months
> stayed sleepless three months
> and they came from Mount Athos
> came from Thessaloniki
> the three enslaved monks.

Like the Dead Sea, we are all
many fathoms below the surface of the Aegean.
Come with me and I will show you the setting:

> In the Dead Sea
> there are no fish
> there is no seaweed
> nor any sea-urchins

there is no life.
There are no creatures
that have a belly
to suffer hunger
that nourish nerves
to suffer pain,
THIS IS THE PLACE, GENTLEMEN!

In the Dead Sea
scornfulness
is no one's trade
no one's worry.
Heart and thought
congeal in salt
that's full of bitterness
and finally join
the mineral world,
THIS IS THE PLACE, GENTLEMEN!

In the Dead Sea
enemies and friends
wife and children
other relations
go and find them.
They're in Gomorrah
down on the bottom
very happy
they don't expect
any message.
GENTLEMEN,

we continue our tour
many fathoms below the surface of the Aegean.

*July '42*

# Calligraphy

*Nile, 'Casino des Pigeons'*

Sails on the Nile,
songless birds with one wing
searching silently for the other;
groping in the sky's absence
for the body of a marble youth;
inscribing on the blue with invisible ink
a desperate cry.

## Days of April '43

Trumpets, trams, cars backfiring, screeching brakes
chloroform his mind in the same way as one counts
so long as one holds out before being lost
in numbness, at the surgeon's mercy.

In the streets he walks carefully, not to slip
on melon-rinds thrown by indifferent Arabs
or refugee politicians and the clique;
they watch him: will he step on it? – will he not?
As one plucks a daisy.
                        He walks on
swinging an enormous bunch of useless keys;
the dry sky recalls
faded advertisements of the Greek Coastal Steamship
        Company,
windows locked on faces one loves
or a little clear water at the root of a plane tree.

He walks on, going to his work, while
a thousand starving dogs tear his trousers to shreds
and strip him naked.
He walks on, staggering, pointed at,
and a dense wind whirls around him
garbage, dung, stench and slander.

*Cairo – Saria Emad-el-Din, 24 June '43*

# Here Among the Bones

Among the bones
music:
it crosses the sand,
crosses the sea.
Among the bones
a flute's sound
the distant sound of a drum
and the faint ringing of bells
crosses the dry fields
crosses the dolphined sea.
High mountains, can't you hear us?
Help! Help!
High mountains, we will dissolve, dead among the dead!

*Cairo, August '43*

## Last Stop

Few are the moonlit nights that I've cared for.
You can read the abecedary of the stars more clearly,
spelling it out
so far as your fatigue at the day's end allows,
extracting new meanings and new hopes.
Now that I sit here, idle, and think about it,
few are the moons that remain in my memory:
islands, colour of a grieving Virgin, late in the waning
or moonlight in northern cities sometimes casting
over turbulent streets, rivers and limbs of men
a heavy torpor.
Yet here last evening, in this our final port
where we wait for the hour of our return home to dawn
like an old debt, like money lying for years
in a miser's safe, and at last
the time for payment comes
and you hear the coins falling onto the table;
in this Etruscan village, behind the sea of Salerno
behind the harbours of our return, on the edge
of an autumn squall, the moon
outstripped the clouds, and houses
on the slope opposite became enamel.
Friendly silences of the moon.

This is a train of thought, a way
to begin to speak of things you confess
uneasily, at times when you can't hold back, to a friend
who escaped secretly and who brings
word from home and from the companions,
and you hurry to open your heart
before exile forestalls you and alters him.

We come from Arabia, Egypt, Palestine, Syria;
the little state
of Kommagene, which flickered out like a small lamp,
often comes to mind,
and great cities that lived for thousands of years
and then became pastures for cattle,
fields for sugar-cane and corn.
We come from the sands of the desert, from the seas of
    Proteus,
souls shrivelled by public sins,
each holding office like a bird in its cage.
The rainy autumn in this gorge
festers the wound of each of us
or what you might term otherwise: nemesis, fate,
or, more simply, bad habits, fraud and deceit,
or even the selfish urge to reap reward from the blood
    of others.
Man frays easily in wars;
man is soft, a sheaf of grass,
lips and fingers that hunger for a white breast
eyes that half-close in the radiance of day
and feet that would run, no matter how tired,
at the slightest call of profit.
Man is soft and thirsty like grass,
insatiable like grass, his nerves roots that spread;
when the harvest comes
he would rather have the scythes whistle in some other field;
when the harvest comes
some call out to exorcize the demon
some become entangled in their riches, others deliver
    speeches.
But what good are exorcisms, riches, speeches
when the living are not there?

Is not man perhaps something else?
Is he not that which transmits life?
A time to plant, a time to harvest.


'The same thing over and over again,' you'll tell me, friend.
But the thinking of a refugee, the thinking of a prisoner,
      the thinking
of a person when he too has become a commodity –
try to change it; you can't.
Maybe he would have liked to stay king of the cannibals
wasting strength that nobody buys,
to promenade in fields of agapanthi
to hear the drums with bamboo overhead,
as courtiers dance with prodigious masks.
But the country they're chopping up and burning like a
      pine tree – you see it
either in the dark train, without water, the windows
      broken, night after night
or in the burning ship that according to the statistics is
      bound to sink –
this is rooted in the mind and doesn't change
this has planted images like those trees
that cast their branches in virgin forests
so that they rivet themselves in the earth and sprout again;
they cast their branches that sprout again, striding mile
      after mile;
our mind's a virgin forest of murdered friends.
And if I talk to you in fables and parables
it's because it's more gentle for you that way; and horror
really can't be talked about because it's alive,
because it's mute and goes on growing:

memory-wounding pain
drips by day drips in sleep.

To speak of heroes to speak of heroes: Michael
who left the hospital with his wounds still open,
perhaps he was speaking of heroes – the night
he dragged his foot through the darkened city –
when he howled, groping over our pain: 'We advance in
    the dark,
we move forward in the dark . . . '
Heroes move forward in the dark.

Few are the moonlit nights that I care for.

*Cava dei Tirreni, 5 October '44*

# 'Thrush'

Ephemeral issue of a vicious daemon and a harsh fate, why do you force me to speak of things that it would be better for you not to know.

– Silenus to Midas

# 'Thrush'

### I

*The house near the sea*

The houses I had they took away from me. The times
happened to be unpropitious: war, destruction, exile;
sometimes the hunter hits the migratory birds,
sometimes he doesn't hit them. Hunting
was good in my time, many felt the pellet;
the rest circle aimlessly or go mad in the shelters.

Don't talk to me about the nightingale or the lark
or the little wagtail
inscribing figures with his tail in the light;
I don't know much about houses
I know they have their own nature, nothing else.
New at first, like babies
who play in gardens with the tassels of the sun,
they embroider coloured shutters and shining doors
over the day.
When the architect's finished, they change,
they frown or smile or even grow resentful
with those who stayed behind, with those who went away
with others who'd come back if they could
or others who disappeared, now that the world's become
an endless hotel.

I don't know much about houses,
I remember their joy and their sorrow
sometimes, when I stop to think;
                              again
sometimes, near the sea, in naked rooms

with a single iron bed and nothing of my own,
watching the evening spider, I imagine
that someone is getting ready to come, that they dress
    him up
in white and black robes, with many-coloured jewels,
and around him venerable ladies,
grey hair and dark lace shawls, talk softly,
that he is getting ready to come and say goodbye to me;
or that a woman – eyelashes quivering, slim-waisted,
returning from southern ports,
Smyrna Rhodes Syracuse Alexandria,
from cities closed like hot shutters,
with perfume of golden fruit and herbs –
climbs the stairs without seeing
those who've fallen asleep under the stairs.

Houses, you know, grow resentful easily when you strip
    them bare.

II

*Sensual Elpenor*

I saw him yesterday standing by the door
below my window; it was about
seven o'clock; there was a woman with him.
He had the look of Elpenor just before he fell
and smashed himself, yet he wasn't drunk.
He was speaking fast, and she
was gazing absently towards the gramophones;
now and then she cut him short to say a word
and then would glance impatiently
towards where they were frying fish: like a cat.
He muttered with a dead cigarette-butt between his lips:

– 'Listen. There's this too. In the moonlight
the statues sometimes bend like reeds
in the midst of ripe fruit – the statues;
and the flame becomes a cool oleander,
the flame that burns one, I mean.'

– 'It's just the light . . . shadows of the night.'

– 'Maybe the night that split open, a blue pomegranate,
a dark breast, and filled you with stars,
cleaving time.
              And yet the statues
bend sometimes, dividing desire in two,
like a peach; and the flame
becomes a kiss on the limbs, then a sob,
then a cool leaf carried off by the wind;
they bend; they become light with a human weight.
You don't forget it.'

- 'The statues are in the museum.'

- 'No, they pursue you, why can't you see it?
I mean with their broken limbs,
with their shape from another time, a shape you don't
        recognize
yet know.
                    It's as though
in the last days of your youth you loved
a woman who was still beautiful, and you were always
        afraid,
as you held her naked at noon,
of the memory aroused by your embrace;
were afraid the kiss might betray you
to other beds now of the past
which nevertheless could haunt you
so easily, so easily, and bring to life
images in the mirror, bodies once alive:
their sensuality.
                    It's as though
returning home from some foreign country you happen
        to open
an old trunk that's been locked up a long time
and find the tatters of clothes you used to wear
on happy occasions, at festivals with many-coloured lights,
mirrored, now becoming dim,
and all that remains is the perfume of the absence
of a young form.
                        Really, those statues are not
the fragments. You yourself are the relic;
they haunt you with a strange virginity
at home, at the office, at receptions for the celebrated,
in the unconfessed terror of sleep;
they speak of things you wish didn't exist

or would happen years after your death,
and that's difficult because . . . '

                 – 'The statues are in the museum.
Good night.'

     – ' . . . because the statues are no longer
fragments. We are. The statues bend lightly . . . Good night.'

At this point they separated. He took
the road leading uphill toward the North
and she moved on towards the light-flooded beach
where the waves are drowned in the noise from the radio:

                       *The radio*

– 'Sails puffed out by the wind
are all that stay in the mind.
Perfume of silence and pine
will soon be an anodyne
now that the sailor's set sail,
flycatcher, catfish and wagtail.
O woman whose touch is dumb,
hear the wind's requiem.

'Drained is the golden keg
the sun's become a rag
round a middle-aged woman's neck
who coughs and coughs without break;
for the summer that's gone she sighs,
for the gold on her shoulders, her thighs.
O woman, O sightless thing,
hear the blind man sing.

'Close the shutters: the day recedes;
make flutes from yesteryear's reeds
and don't open, knock how they may:
they shout but have nothing to say.
Take cyclamen, pine-needles, the lily,
anemones out of the sea;
O woman whose wits are lost,
listen, the water's ghost . . .

– 'Athens. The public has heard
the news with alarm; it is feared
a crisis is near. The prime
minister declared: "There is no more time . . .
Take cyclamen . . . needles of pine . . .
the lily . . . needles of pine . . .
O woman . . .
– . . . is overwhelmingly stronger.
The war . . . '
                    SOULMONGER.

III

*The wreck* 'Thrush'

'This wood that cooled my forehead
at times when noon burned my veins
will flower in other hands. Take it. I'm giving it to you;
look, it's wood from a lemon tree...'
                                          I heard the voice
as I was gazing at the sea trying to make out
a ship they'd sunk there years ago;
it was called '*Thrush*', a small wreck; the masts,
broken, swayed at odd angles deep underwater, like tentacles,
or the memory of dreams, marking the hull:
vague mouth of some huge dead sea-monster
extinguished in the water. Calm spread all around.

And gradually, in turn, other voices followed,
whispers thin and thirsty
emerging from the other side of the sun, the dark side;
you might say they were asking to drink a drop of blood;
familiar voices, but I couldn't distinguish one from the
      other.
And then the voice of the old man reached me; I felt it
falling into the heart of day,
quietly, as though motionless:
'And if you condemn me to drink poison, I thank you.
Your law will be my law; how can I go
wandering from one foreign country to another, a rolling
      stone.
I prefer death.
Whose path is for the better only God knows.'

◆

Countries of the sun yet you cannot face the sun.
Countries of men yet you cannot face man.


*The light*

As the years go by
the judges who condemn you grow in number;
as the years go by and you converse with fewer voices,
you see the sun with different eyes:
you know that those who stayed behind were deceiving you
the delirium of flesh, the lovely dance
that ends in nakedness.
It's as though, turning at night into an empty highway,
you suddenly see the eyes of an animal shine,
eyes already gone; so you feel your own eyes:
you gaze at the sun, then you're lost in darkness.
The Doric chiton
that swayed like the mountains when your fingers touched it
is a marble figure in the light, but its head is in darkness.
And those who abandoned the stadium to take up arms
struck the obstinate marathon runner
and he saw the track sail in blood,
the world empty like the moon,
the gardens of victory wither:
you see them in the sun, behind the sun.
And the boys who dived from the bowsprits
go like spindles twisting still,
naked bodies plunging into black light
with a coin between the teeth, swimming still,
while the sun with golden needles sews
sails and wet wood and colours of the sea;

even now they're going down obliquely
toward the pebbles on the sea floor,
white oil-flasks.

Light, angelic and black,
laughter of waves on the sea's highways,
tear-stained laughter,
the old suppliant sees you
as he moves to cross the invisible fields –
light mirrored in his blood,
the blood that gave birth to Eteocles and Polynices.
Day, angelic and black;
the brackish taste of woman that poisons the prisoner
emerges from the wave a cool branch adorned with drops.
Sing little Antigone, sing, O sing . . .
I'm not speaking to you about things past, I'm speaking
      about love;
adorn your hair with the sun's thorns,
dark girl;
the heart of the Scorpion has set,
the tyrant in man has fled,
and all the daughters of the sea, Nereids, Graeae,
hurry toward the shimmering of the rising goddess:
whoever has never loved will love,
in the light;
                  and you find yourself
in a large house with many windows open
running from room to room, not knowing from where to
      look out first,
because the pine trees will vanish, and the mirrored
      mountains, and the chirping of birds
the sea will empty, shattered glass, from north and south

your eyes will empty of the light of day
the way the cicadas all together suddenly fall silent.

*Poros, 'Galini', 31 October 1946*

# Logbook III

*To the People of Cyprus,*
*in Memory and Love*

'. . . Cyprus, where it was decreed
by Apollo that I should live . . . '

# Agianapa I

And you see the light of the sun, as the ancients used to say.
And yet I thought I was seeing all these years
walking between the mountains and the sea
coming across men in perfect armour;
strange, I didn't notice that I saw their voices only.
It was the blood that forced them to talk, the ram
that I slaughtered and spread at their feet;
but that red carpet was not the light.
Whatever they told me I had to recognize by touch
as when they hide you at night, hunted, in a stable
or when you finally attain the body of a full-breasted
        woman
and the room is thick with suffocating odours;
whatever they told me: fur and silk.

Strange, here I see the light of the sun; the gold net
where things quiver like fish
that a huge angel draws in
along with the nets of the fishermen.

## Dream

I sleep and my heart stays awake;
it gazes at the stars, the sky and the helm,
and at how the water blossoms on the rudder.

# Details on Cyprus

*To the painter Diamandí*

The little owl was always there
perched on the doorkey to St Máma,
given blindly to the honey of the sun
here or elsewhere, now, in the past:
it danced to that kind of rhythm in autumn.
Angels unwound the heavens
and a stone figure with arched eyebrows
stared idly from a corner of the roof.

Then the monk appeared: skull-cap, frock, leather belt,
and went to work decorating the gourd.
He began at the neck: palm trees, fish-scales, rings.
Then, cupping its round belly with a broad palm,
he added the cheating farmer, the cheating merchant, the
        cheating miller and the slanderer;
then the infant-hater and the defrocked nun;
and at the bottom, almost hidden, the sleepless worm.

All this was fine, a casual stroll.
But the wooden well-wheel – the 'alakátin' –
asleep in the shade of the walnut tree
half in the earth and half in the water,
why did you try to wake it?
You saw how it moaned. And that cry,
brought forth from the wood's ancient nerves,
why did you call it the voice of our country?

## In the Goddess's Name I Summon You.

Oil on limbs,
maybe a rancid smell
as on the chapel's
oil-press here,
as on the rough pores
of the unturning stone.

Oil on hair
wreathed in rope
and maybe other scents
unknown to us
poor and rich
and statuettes offering
small breasts with their fingers.

Oil in the sun
the leaves shuddered
when the stranger stopped
and the silence weighed
between the knees.
The coins fell:
'In the goddess's name I summon you...'

Oil on the shoulders
and the flexing waist
legs grass-dappled,
and that wound in the sun
as the bell rang for vespers
as I spoke in the churchyard
with a crippled man.

# Helen

TEUCER:   ... *in sea-girt Cyprus, where it was decreed*
*by Apollo that I should live, giving the city*
*the name of Salamis in memory of my island home.*

.   .   .   .   .   .   .   .   .   .   .

HELEN:   *I never went to Troy; it was a phantom.*

.   .   .   .   .   .   .   .   .   .   .

SERVANT:   *What? You mean it was only for a cloud*
*that we struggled so much?*

— EURIPIDES, *HELEN*


'The nightingales won't let you sleep in Platres.'

Shy nightingale, in the breathing of the leaves,
you who bestow the forest's musical coolness
on the sundered bodies, on the souls
of those who know they will not return.
Blind voice, you who grope in the darkness of memory
for footsteps and gestures — I wouldn't dare say kisses —
and the bitter raving of the frenzied slave-woman.

'The nightingales won't let you sleep in Platres.'

Platres: where is Platres? And this island: who knows it?
I've lived my life hearing names I've never heard before:
new countries, new idiocies of men
or of the gods;
                    my fate, which wavers
between the last sword of some Ajax
and another Salamis,
brought me here, to this shore.
                              The moon
rose from the sea like Aphrodite,

covered the Archer's stars, now moves to find
the heart of Scorpio, and alters everything.
Truth, where's the truth?
I too was an archer in the war;
my fate: that of a man who missed his target.

Lyric nightingale,
on a night like this, by the shore of Proteus,
the Spartan slave-girls heard you and began their lament,
and among them – who would have believed it? – Helen!
She whom we hunted so many years by the banks of the
      Scamander.
She was there, at the desert's lip; I touched her; she spoke
      to me:
'It isn't true, it isn't true,' she cried.
'I didn't board the blue-bowed ship.
I never went to valiant Troy.'

Breasts girded high, the sun in her hair, and that stature
shadows and smiles everywhere,
on shoulders, thighs and knees;
the skin alive, and her eyes
with the large eyelids,
she was there, on the banks of a Delta.
                                        And at Troy?
At Troy, nothing: just a phantom image.
That's how the gods wanted it.
And Paris, Paris lay with a shadow as though it were a solid
      being;
and for ten whole years we slaughtered ourselves for Helen.

Great suffering had desolated Greece.
So many bodies thrown
into the jaws of the sea, the jaws of the earth

so many souls
fed to the millstones like grain.
And the rivers swelling, blood in their silt,
all for a linen undulation, a filmy cloud,
a butterfly's flicker, a wisp of swan's down,
an empty tunic – all for a Helen.
And my brother?
                                        Nightingale nightingale nightingale,
what is a god? What is not a god? And what is there in
    between them?


'The nightingales won't let you sleep in Platres.'


Tearful bird,
                    on sea-kissed Cyprus
consecrated to remind me of my country,
I moored alone with this fable,
if it's true that it is a fable,
if it's true that mortals will not again take up
the old deceit of the gods;
                                        if it's true
that in future years some other Teucer,
or some Ajax or Priam or Hecuba,
or someone unknown and nameless who nevertheless saw
a Scamander overflow with corpses,
isn't fated to hear
messengers coming to tell him
that so much suffering, so much life,
went into the abyss
all for an empty tunic, all for a Helen.

## Memory I

*And there was no more sea*

And I with only a reed in my hands.
The night was deserted, the moon waning,
earth smelled of the last rain.
I whispered: memory hurts wherever you touch it,
there's only a little sky, there's no more sea,
what they kill by day they carry away in carts and dump
        behind the ridge.

My fingers were running idly over this flute
that an old shepherd gave to me because I said good evening
        to him.
The others have abolished every kind of greeting:
they wake, shave, and start the day's work of slaughter
as one prunes or operates, methodically, without passion;
sorrow's dead like Patroclus, and no one makes a mistake.

I thought of playing a tune and then I felt ashamed in front
        of the other world
the one that watches me from beyond the night from within
        my light
woven of living bodies, naked hearts
and love that belongs to the Furies
as it belongs to man and to stone and to water and to grass
and to the animal that looks straight into the eye of its
        approaching death.

So I continued along the dark path
and turned into my garden and dug and buried the reed

and again I whispered: some morning the resurrection will
    come,
dawn's light will glow red as trees blossom in spring,
the sea will be born again, and the wave will again fling
    forth Aphrodite.
We are the seed that dies. And I entered my empty house.

## The Demon of Fornication

> ... *Nicosia e Famagosta*
> *per la lor bestia si lamenti e garra* ...
>   — Paradiso

> ... *even as you know that the demon of fornication*
> *assails the whole world, so he beguiled the king,*
> *and the good king fell into sin* ...
>   — Chronicle of Makhairas

Juan Visconti had written the truth.
How the Count of Rochas had pimps in his pay,
how he and the queen were in it together,
how the thing started and how it ended
was hawked in the streets and squares
by every boy in Nicosia.
That the letter he sent to the king in France
was accurate, the counsellors knew well enough.

                                    But now
they had come together to discuss the issue and advise
the Crown of Cyprus and Jerusalem;
now they had been ordered to judge
Queen Eleanora, descended from
a great family among the Catalans;
and the Catalans are merciless men,
so that if the king chose to avenge himself
it would be nothing for the Catalans to take up arms
and come to wipe out every one of them and their fortunes
      too.
Their responsibility was great, terribly great;
the very kingdom depended on their judgement.

•

That Visconti was honest and loyal
of course they knew; but he hurried things,
acted thoughtlessly, indecorously, extravagantly.
The king was irascible – how had Visconti failed
to keep that in mind? – irascible
and prostrate to Eleanora's desire:
her shift always with him when he travelled
so that he could take it in his arms at night;
and impious Visconti went and wrote to him
that they'd found the ram with his ewe –
how can you write a thing like that to a ruler?
He was a fool. At least he should have remembered
that the king too had made mistakes:
pretending to be so enraptured
while two mistresses hovered at the back door.
What an uproar on the island when Eleanora
ordered one of the two – the pregnant one – to be brought
     before her
and had them lay a hand-mill on her belly
to grind out flour measure by measure.
And worst of all – the mind boggles –
when the whole world knows that the king
was born under the sign of Capricorn,
that luckless Visconti takes pen in hand
the very night the moon comes under Capricorn
to write what: about horns and rams!
The prudent man never tempts fate.
No; we aren't sworn to say
where justice lies. Our duty
is to find the lesser of evils.
Better for one man to die because he was fated to,
than for us to put ourselves and the kingdom in danger.

So they argued through the day
and then, towards sunset, they approached the king,
bowed before him and said that Juan Visconti
was an infamous, perverted liar.

And Juan Visconti died of hunger in a dungeon.
But in the king's soul the seed of his shame
spread tentacles, and this made him long
to serve others as he had been served.
No lady but he tried to make a whore of her;
he shamed them all. Fear and hate coupled
and filled the land with fear and hate.

In this way, with the 'lesser evil', fate marched on
until the dawn of St Anthony's day, a Wednesday,
when the knights came and dragged the king
from his mistress's embrace to slaughter him.
'And after all the others came the Turkopolier
and found him lying in his own blood' says the Chronicler,
'and drew his sword and cut his member off
and his testicles, and said to him: For these
you paid with your death!'
                              This was the end
allotted King Peter by the demon of fornication.

# Three Mules

*And the Queen mounted on the wonderful mule*
*called Margarita, which had belonged to her*
*husband King Peter, and she sat upon the*
*wonderful mule as women do; and she ordered her*
*squire who was called Putsurello to bring her spurs*
*with him. And she said to him: 'When I make a*
*sign to you, turn my foot over so that I sit like a*
*man and put on my spurs.'*

        – CHRONICLE OF MAKHAIRAS

*Letter to Mastro*

In Damascus one sleepless night
I saw the shade of Oum Haram pass by,
the venerable kinswoman of the Prophet.
I heard the clatter of hooves like silver dinars,
then I saw her, seemingly crossing hills of salt
towards Larnaca, astride her mule.
I waited there among cool branches
biting the fruit of a myrtle bush;
a whiteness stung my eyes,
maybe the salt, maybe her ghost. And then
in the shrubs, a whisper:
                'It was here
that my animal slipped. This stone
struck the nape of my pellucid neck
and I yielded up my victorious soul.
I was full of the will of God;
a mule can't bear that much weight;
don't forget it, and don't wrong the mule.'

She spoke and disappeared. Yet, even now
her mule still grazes in my mind,
as does that other mule, whose heart stopped dead
when they freed her of the two coffins,
the two brothers unjustly executed
by the hangman there in Koutsovendi.

But the greatest of them all, what can I say of her? In a
    country
where those who lived below the castles
were forgotten like last year's earth,
she still sails free on the wings of fame,
the celebrated beast of Queen Eleanora.
Against her belly, the golden spurs;
on her saddle, those insatiable loins;
at her trotting, those jolting breasts
ripe as pomegranates with murder.
And when Neapolitans, Genoese and Lombards
brought to the royal table
on a silver tray, all bloody,
the shirt of the murdered king
and did in his wretched brother John,
I imagine how she must have neighed that night,
beyond the apathy of her race,
as a dog howls,
rich in trappings, golden-crouped, in the stable,
Margarita the mule.

## Pentheus

Sleep filled him with dreams of fruit and leaves;
wakefulness kept him from picking even a mulberry.
And the two together divided his limbs among the Bacchae.

## Memory II

*Ephesus*

He spoke while sitting on what seemed to be
the marble remnant of an ancient gate;
endless the plain on the right and empty,
on the left the last shadows moved down the mountain:
'The poem is everywhere. Your voice
sometimes travels beside it
like a dolphin keeping company for a while
with a golden sloop in the sunlight,
then vanishing again. The poem is everywhere,
like the wings of the wind moved by the wind
to touch for a moment the sea-gull's wings.
The same as our lives yet different too,
as a woman's face changes yet remains the same
after she strips naked. He who has loved
knows this; in the light that other people see things,
the world spoils; but you remember this:
Hades and Dionysus are the same.'
He spoke and then took the main road
that leads to the old harbour, devoured now
under the rushes there. The twilight
as if ready for the death of some animal,
so naked was it.

I remember still:
he was travelling to Ionian shores, to empty shells of
      theatres
where only the lizard slithers over the dry stones,
and I asked him: 'Will they be full again some day?'
and he answered: 'Maybe, at the hour of death.'
And he ran across the orchestra howling

'Let me hear my brother!'
And the silence surrounding us was harsh,
leaving no trace at all on the glass of the blue.

## Salamis in Cyprus

> ... and Salamis,
> whose mother-city is now
> the cause of our troubles.
>
> – AESCHYLUS, *THE PERSIANS*

Sometimes the midday sun, sometimes handfuls of light
    rain
and the beach covered with fragments of ancient jars.
The columns insignificant; only the church of St Epiphanios
revealing – dark, sunken – the might of the golden Empire.

Young bodies, loved and loving, have passed by here;
throbbing breasts, shells rose-pink, feet
fearlessly skimming the water,
and arms open for the coupling of desire.
The Lord upon many waters,
here upon this crossing.

Then I heard footsteps on the stones.
I didn't see any faces; they'd gone by the time I turned.
But the voice, heavy like the tread of oxen,
remained there in the sky's veins, in the sea's roll
over the pebbles, again and again:

'Earth has no handles
for them to shoulder her and carry her off,
nor can they, however thirsty,
sweeten the sea with half a dram of water.
And those bodies,
formed of a clay they know not,
have souls.
They gather tools to change them;

they won't succeed: they'll only unmake them
if souls can be unmade.
Wheat doesn't take long to ripen,
it doesn't take much time
for the yeast of bitterness to rise,
it doesn't take much time
for evil to raise its head,
and the sick mind emptying
doesn't take much time
to fill with madness:
there is an island . . . '

Friends from the other war,
on this deserted and cloudy beach
I think of you as the day turns –
those who fell fighting and those who fell years after the
    battle,
those who saw dawn through the mist of death
or, in wild solitude under the stars,
felt upon them the huge dark eyes
of total disaster;
and those again who prayed
when flaming steel sawed the ships:
'Lord, help us to keep in mind
the causes of this slaughter:
greed, dishonesty, selfishness,
the desiccation of love;
Lord, help us to root these out . . . '

– Now, on this pebbled beach, it's better to forget;
talking does no good;
who can change the attitude of those with power?
Who can make himself heard?

Each dreams separately without hearing anyone else's
   nightmare.

– True. But the messenger moves swiftly,
and however long his journey, he'll bring
to those who tried to shackle the Hellespont
the terrible news from Salamis.

Voice of the Lord upon the waters.
There is an island.

*Salamis, Cyprus, November '53*

## Euripides the Athenian

He grew old between the fires of Troy
and the quarries of Sicily.

He liked sea-shore caves and pictures of the sea.
He saw the veins of men
as a net the gods made to catch us in like wild beasts:
he tried to break through it.
He was a sour man, his friends were few;
when his time came he was torn to pieces by dogs.

# Engomi

The plain was broad and level; from a distance you could see
arms in motion as they dug.
In the sky, the clouds all curves, here and there
a trumpet gold and rose: the sunset.
In the thin grass and the thorns
a light after-shower breeze stirred: it had rained
there on the peaks of the mountains that now took on colour.

And I moved on toward those at work,
women and men digging with picks in trenches.
It was an ancient city; walls, streets and houses
stood out like the petrified muscles of Cyclopes,
the anatomy of spent strength under the eye
of the archaeologist, anaesthetist or surgeon.
Phantoms and fabrics, luxury and lips, buried
and the curtains of pain spread wide open
to reveal, naked and indifferent, the tomb.

And I looked up toward those at work,
the taut shoulders, the arms that struck
this dead silence with a rhythm heavy and swift
as though the wheel of fate were passing through the ruins.

Suddenly I was walking and did not walk
I looked at the flying birds, and they had stopped stone-dead
I looked at the sky's air, and it was full of wonder
I looked at the bodies labouring, and they were still
and among them a face climbing the light.
The black hair spilled over the collar, the eyebrows
had the motion of a swallow's wings, the nostrils
arched above the lips, and the body

emerged from the struggling arms stripped
with the unripe breasts of the Virgin,
a motionless dance.

And I lowered my eyes to look all around:
girls kneaded, but they didn't touch the dough
women spun, but the spindles didn't turn
lambs were drinking, but their tongues hung still
above green waters that seemed asleep
and the herdsman transfixed with his staff poised.
And I looked again at that body ascending;
people had gathered like ants,
and they struck her with lances but didn't wound her.
Her belly now shone like the moon
and I thought the sky was the womb
that bore her and now took her back, mother and child.
Her feet were still visible, adamantine
then they vanished: an Assumption.
                                    The world
became again as it had been, ours:
the world of time and earth.
                                    Aromas of terebinth
began to stir on the old slopes of memory
breasts among leaves, lips moist;
and all went dry at once on the length of the plain,
in the stone's despair, in eroded power,
in that empty place with the thin grass and the thorns
where a snake slithered heedless,
where they take a long time to die.

*Three Secret Poems*

# On a Ray of Winter Light

### 1

Leaves like rusty tin
for the desolate mind that has seen the end –
the barest glimmerings.
Leaves aswirl with gulls
frenzied by winter.

The way the heart finds release
the dancers turned into trees,
into a huge forest of trees stripped bare.

### 2

White seaweed burns,
grey-haired sea-nymphs, eyes lidless, rise from the waves –
shapes that once danced,
flames now crystallized.
Snow has covered the world.

### 3

My companions had driven me mad
with theodolites, sextants, lodestones,
with telescopes that enlarge things –
better if they kept at a distance.
Where will roads like these lead us?
But maybe the day that began then
has not yet died out
with a rose-like fire in a ravine,
with a sea ethereal at the feet of God.

4

Years ago you said:
'Essentially I'm a matter of light.'
And still today when you lean
on the broad shoulders of sleep
or even when they anchor you
to the sea's drowsy breast
you look for crannies where the blackness
has worn thin and has no resistance,
groping you search for the lance –
the lance destined to pierce your heart
and lay it open to the light.

5

What turbid river took us under?
We stayed in the depths.
The current flows above our heads,
bending inarticulate reeds;

the voices
under the chestnut tree turned into pebbles –
pebbles that children throw.

6

A breath of air, then another, a gust
as you put down the book
and tear up useless bygone papers
or lean forward to watch in the meadow
arrogant centaurs galloping
or nubile Amazons with sweat

in all the runnels of the body
as they compete at jumping and wrestling.

Gusts of resurrection one dawn
when you thought it was the sun that had risen.


7

Flame is healed by flame,
not in the slow trickle of moments
but in a single flash, at once;
like the longing that merged with another longing
so that the two remained riveted
or like
the rhythm in music that stays
there at the centre like a statue

immovable.

This breath of life is not a transition:
the thunderbolt rules it.

## On Stage

### 1

Sun, you are playing with me
but this is no dance –
such extreme nakedness
is blood almost,
or some savage forest;
then . . .

### 2

Gongs were heard
and the messengers arrived –
I wasn't expecting them,
even the way they spoke beyond recollection –
rested, their clothes freshly changed,
carrying fruit in baskets.
I was amazed and whispered:
'I love these amphitheatres.'
The concave shell filled immediately
and on the stage the light dimmed
as though for some celebrated murder.

### 3

What were you after? Your look a stammer.
You had just woken up
leaving the sheets to grow ice-cold
and the baths of revenge.
Drops of water ran down your shoulders,
over your belly,

your feet bare on the soil,
on the cut grass.
The others, three –
the faces of brazen Hecate –
tried to take you with them.
Your eyes were two tragic shells,
two small purple stones
covered your nipples –
stage properties perhaps.
The three bellowed,
you stood rooted to the soil.
Their gesticulations rent the air.
Slaves brought them knives,
you stood rooted to the soil,
a cypress.
They drew the knives from the sheaths,
looked for a place to stab you.
Only then did you cry out:
'Let anyone come and sleep with me who wants to:
am I not the sea?'


4

The sea: how did the sea get like this?
I lingered for years in the mountains;
the fireflies blinded me.
Now, on this beach,
I'm waiting for someone to land,
or a piece of flotsam, a raft.

But is it possible for the sea to fester?
A dolphin once cut through it,
as did once
the tip of a gull's wing.

Yet the sea was sweet
wherever I plunged in and swam as a child,
and later, as a young man,
while searching for shapes in the pebbles,
trying to discover rhythms,
the Old Sea-god said to me:
'I am the place you belong to;
I may be nobody,
but I can become that which you need.'

. 5

Who heard, at the stroke of noon,
the knife hiss on the whetstone?
What rider was it that came
with kindling, with a firebrand?
Everyone washes his hands,
cools them.
And who disembowelled
the woman, the child, the house?
There's no culprit, not a trace.
Who fled,
horseshoes striking the flagstones?
They have annihilated their eyes, gone blind.
There are no witnesses now, to anything.

6

When will you speak again?
Our words are the children of many people.
They are sown, are born like infants,
take root, are nourished with blood.
As pine trees
hold the wind's imprint

after the wind has gone, is no longer there,
so words
retain a man's imprint
after the man has gone, is no longer there.
Perhaps the stars are trying to speak,
those that stamped your great nakedness one night –
the Swan, the Archer, the Scorpion –
perhaps those.
But where will you be the moment
the light comes, here, to this theatre?


7

Yet there, on the other shore,
under the cave's black stare,
suns in your eyes, birds on your shoulders,
you were there; you suffered
the other labour, love,
the other dawn, the reappearance
the other birth, the resurrection.
Yet there, in the vast dilation of time,
you were remade
drop by drop, like resin,
like the stalactite, the stalagmite.

## Summer Solstice

### 1

On one side the sun at its grandest,
on the other the new moon,
distant in memory like those breasts.
Between them the chasm of a night full of stars,
life's deluge.
The horses on the threshing-floors
gallop and sweat
over scattered bodies.
Everything finds its way there,
and this woman
whom you saw when she was beautiful, suddenly
sags, gives way, kneels.
The millstones grind up everything
and everything turns into stars.

Eve of the longest day.

### 2

Everyone sees visions
but no one admits to it;
they continue to live thinking they're alone.
The huge rose
was always here
beside you, sunk deep in sleep,
yours and unknown.
But only now that your lips have touched
its innermost petals
have you known the dancer's dense weight

fall into time's river –
the terrible splash.

Don't dissipate the vitality
that this breath of life has given you.


### 3

Yet in sleep of this kind
dreams degenerate so readily
into nightmares.
Like a fish gleaming under the waves,
then burying itself in the slimy depths,
or the chameleon when it changes colour.
In the city now turned into a brothel
pimps and whores
hawk putrid charms;
the girl who rose from the sea
puts on a cow's hide
to make the bull-calf mount her;
as for the poet –
urchins pelt him with turds
while he watches the statues dripping blood.
You've got to break out of this sleep,
out of this flagellated skin.


### 4

Litter swirls
in the mad scattering wind
right left, up down.
Fine lethal fumes
dissolve men's limbs.
Souls

longing to leave the body
thirst, but they can't find water anywhere:
they stick here, stick there, haphazardly,
birds caught in lime –
in vain they struggle
until their wings fail completely.

This place – earthen pitcher –
gets drier and drier.


5

This world wrapped in soporific sheets
has nothing to offer
but this ending.
                    In the hot night
Hecate's withered priestess
up on the roof, breasts bared,
supplicates an artificial full moon,
while two adolescent slave-girls, yawning,
mix aromatic potions
in a large copper pot.
Those who relish perfumes will have their fill tomorrow.

Her passion and her make-up
are those of the tragic actress –
their plaster has peeled off already.


6

Down among the laurels,
down among the white oleanders,
down on the jagged rock,
the sea like glass at our feet.

Remember the tunic that you saw
come open, slip down over nakedness,
fall around the ankles,
dead –
if only this sleep had fallen like that
among the laurels of the dead.


7

The poplar's breathing in the little garden
measures your time
day and night –
a water-clock filled by the sky.
In strong moonlight its leaves
trail black footprints across the white wall.
Along the border the pine trees are few,
and beyond, marble and beams of light
and people the way people are made.
Yet the blackbird sings
when it comes to drink
and sometimes you hear the turtle-dove's call.

In the little garden – this tiny patch –
you can see the light of the sun
striking two red carnations,
an olive tree and a bit of honeysuckle.
Accept who you are.
                    Don't
drown the poem in deep plane trees;
nurture it with what earth and rock you have.
For things beyond this –
to find them dig in this same place.

8

The white sheet of paper, harsh mirror,
gives back only what you were.

The white sheet talks with your voice,
your very own,
not the voice you'd like to have;
your music is life,
the life you wasted.
If you want to, you can regain it:
concentrate on this blank object
that throws you back
to where you started.

You travelled, saw many moons, many suns,
touched dead and living,
felt the pain young men know,
the wailing of women,
a boy's bitterness –
what you've felt will fall away to nothing
unless you commit yourself to this void.
Maybe you'll find there what you thought was lost:
youth's burgeoning, the justified shipwreck of age.

Your life is what you gave,
this void is what you gave:
the white sheet of paper.

9

You spoke about things they couldn't see
and so they laughed.

Yet to row up the dark river
against the current,
to take the unknown road
blindly, stubbornly,
and to search for words rooted
like the knotted olive tree –
let them laugh.
And to yearn for the other world to inhabit
today's suffocating loneliness,
this ravaged present –
let them be.

The sea-breeze and the freshness of dawn
exist whether or not we want them to.


10

At that time of dawn
when dreams come true
I saw lips opening
petal by petal.

A slender sickle shone in the sky.
I was afraid it might cut them down.

### 11

The sea that they call tranquillity,
ships and white sails,
the breeze off the pine trees and Aegina's mountain,
panting breath;
your skin glided over her skin,
easy and warm,
thought barely formed and forgotten at once.

But in the shallow sea
a speared octopus spurted ink,
and in the depths –
only consider how far down the beautiful islands go.

I looked at you with all the light and the darkness I possess.

### 12

The blood surges now
as heat swells
the veins of the inflamed sky.
It is trying to go beyond death,
to discover joy.

The light is a pulse
beating ever more slowly
as though about to stop.

13

Soon now the sun will stop.
Dawn's ghosts
have blown into the dry shells;
a bird sang three times, three times only;
the lizard on a white stone
motionless
stares at the parched grass
where a tree-snake slithered away.
A black wing makes a deep gash
high in the sky's blue dome –
look at it, you'll see it break open.

Birth-pang of resurrection.


14

Now
with the lead melted for divination,
with the brilliance of the summer sea,
all life's nakedness,
the transition and the standing still, the subsidence and the
        upsurge,
the lips, the gently touched skin –
all are longing to burn.

As the pine tree at the stroke of noon
mastered by resin
strains to bring forth flame
and can't endure the pangs any longer –

summon the children to gather the ash,
to sow it.

Everything that has passed has fittingly passed.
And even what has not yet passed
must burn
this noon when the sun is riveted
to the heart of the multipetalled rose.

*from*

# *Book of Exercises II*

# Letter to Rex Warner

*Resident of Storrs, Connecticut, U.S.A.*
*On his Sixtieth Birthday*

At the time we met
you were telling the story of the wild goose chase
in the Kingdom of hermaphrodites;
there the football field
had witnessed barefaced slaughter.
I was returning from a marble stadium
where the obstinate marathon runner, wounded,
saw the track sailing in blood.
That way I sensed who you were and we became friends.

We were in a country devastated by the war –
they'd crippled even the dolls of children.
The light, quick and strong,
bit into everything, turned it to stone.
We walked among bicycles and kites,
watched the colours, but our talk
strayed to that festering horror.

Years went by and I found you again
on soil lush with vegetation,
where poison ivy sometimes lies in wait
and studious children learn
to unravel wise books
and the labyrinth of love.
You always celebrated Homer and his breed.
A squirrel – spasmodic circumflex –
climbed higher and higher up a giant tree

and you watched it
laughing.

Our life is always a separation
and a more difficult presence.

Now, in this many-tentacled city,
I think about you once again.
Everything's television,
you can't touch things easily at close quarters.
In the heat of this electric night,
in the unbroken loneliness of the sea floor,
the luminous skyscrapers
show their windows gleaming
like the skin of a huge sea-monster
as it breaks clear of the waves.
The many-coloured people filling them,
countless jostling people,
were leaving at this time
for other pleasures, other anxieties.
They were emptied – not a soul remaining –
like the multicelled nests of that sparrow
called philetaerus
– *Philetaerus Socius*;
you find them in the thorny acacia
or in the museum, if you look for them.
'I grieve for the gourd'
murmured the prophet Jonah
gazing at the great city of Nineveh.
His words turn the mind
toward the wakeful dreams
it gathered during its day's work:
bulls and horses with mouths wide open
and tongues like sudden daggers;

an immigrant El Greco like the pit of hell
speaking a language
incomprehensible to everyone;
and that sculptor
who believed the sky was red
and struggled with the voracious space
that was devouring the sculpture in his hands:
smaller and smaller still and thinner
to the point of nothingness.
They've sunk out of sight, those years that gallant young
        Megacles,
the athlete's oil-flask hanging from his left arm,
went and offered Persephone with such tenderness
the pomegranate he was holding
in his three fingers.

Now you are sixty
and I can't offer you anything
except this idle chirping.
Still, I feel that I'm encircled and goaded on
by a dense flock of philetaerus sparrows.


*New York, N.Y., June 1965 –*
*Princeton, N.J., Winter 1968*

## The Cats of St Nicholas

> *But deep inside me sings*
> *the Fury's lyreless threnody;*
> *my heart, self-taught, has lost*
> *the precious confidence of hope . . .*
>
> – AESCHYLUS, *AGAMEMNON* 990 ff.


'That's the Cape of Cats ahead,' the captain said to me,
pointing through the mist to a low stretch of shore,
the beach deserted; it was Christmas Day –
'. . . and there, in the distance to the west, is where
     Aphrodite rose out of the waves;
they call the place "Greek's Rock".
Left ten degrees rudder!'
She had Salome's eyes, the cat I lost a year ago;
and old Ramazan, how he would look death square in
     the eyes,
whole days long in the snow of the East,
under the frozen sun,
days long square in the eyes: the young hearth god.
Don't stop, traveller.
'Left ten degrees rudder,' muttered the helmsman.


. . . my friend, though, might well have stopped,
now between ships,
shut up in a small house with pictures,
searching for windows behind the frames.
The ship's bell struck
like a coin from some vanished city
that brings to mind, as it falls,
alms from another time.
'It's strange,' the captain said.
'That bell – given what day it is –
reminded me of another, the monastery bell.

A monk told me the story,
a half-mad monk, a kind of dreamer.

'It was during the great drought,
forty years without rain,
the whole island devastated,
people died and snakes were born.
This cape had millions of snakes
thick as a man's legs
and full of poison.
In those days the monastery of St Nicholas
was held by the monks of St Basil,
and they couldn't work their fields,
couldn't put their flocks to pasture.
In the end they were saved by the cats they raised.
Every day at dawn a bell would strike
and an army of cats would move into battle.
They'd fight the day long,
until the bell sounded for the evening feed.
Supper done, the bell would sound again
and out they'd go to battle through the night.
They say it was a marvellous sight to see them,
some lame, some blind, others missing
a nose, an ear, their hides in shreds.
So to the sound of four bells a day
months went by, years, season after season.
Wildly obstinate, always wounded,
they annihilated the snakes but in the end disappeared:
they just couldn't take in that much poison.
Like a sunken ship
they left no trace on the surface:
not a miaow, not a bell even.
Steady as you go!
                    Poor devils, what could they do,

fighting like that day and night, drinking
the poisonous blood of those snakes?
Generations of poison, centuries of poison.'
'Steady as you go,' indifferently echoed the helmsman.

*Wednesday, 5 February 1969*

## 'On Aspalathoi . . .'

Sounion was lovely that spring day –
the Feast of the Annunciation.
Sparse green leaves around rust-coloured stone,
red earth, and aspalathoi
with their huge thorns and their yellow flowers
already out.
In the distance the ancient columns, strings of a harp still
    vibrating . . .

Peace.
– What could have made me think of Ardiaios?
Possibly a word in Plato, buried in the mind's furrows:
the name of the yellow bush
hasn't changed since his time.
That evening I found the passage:
'They bound him hand and foot,' it says,
'they flung him down and flayed him,
they dragged him along
gashing his flesh on thorny aspalathoi,
and they went and threw him into Tartarus, torn to shreds.'

In this way Ardiaios, the terrible Pamphylian tyrant,
paid for his crimes in the nether world.

*31 March 1971*

APPENDIX

*Rhymed Poems*

(1924–1953)

# Turning Point

Σὴν χάριν

# SHELLS, CLOUDS

But everything went wrong for me and upside down,
the nature of things was reborn for me.

– *The Erotokritos*

# Turning Point

Moment, sent by a hand
I had loved so much,
you reached me just at sunset
like a black pigeon.

The road whitened before me,
soft breath of sleep
at the close of a last supper . . .
Moment, grain of sand,

alone you kept the whole
tragic clepsydra dumb,
as though it had seen the Hydra
in the heavenly garden.

## Slowly You Spoke

Slowly you spoke before the sun
and now it's dark
and you were my fate's woof
you, whom they'd call Billio.

Five seconds; and what's happened
in the wide world?
An unwritten love rubbed out
and a dry pitcher

and it's dark . . . Where is the place
and your nakedness to the waist,
my God, and my favourite spot
and the style of your soul!

# The Sorrowing Girl

On the stone of patience
you sat at nightfall,
the black of your eye
revealing your pain;

on your lips the line
that's naked and trembles
when the soul spins
and sobs plead;

in your mind the motive
that starts tears
and you were a body that from the verge
returns to fruitfulness;

but your heart's anguish
didn't cry out, became
what gives the world
a star-filled sky.

## Automobile

On the highway like the forked embrace
of a pair of compasses,
fingers of wind in the hair
and miles in the belly,

the two of us were leaving, empty,
whiplash for the mild gaze;
the mind make-up, the blood make-up
naked, naked, naked!

*. . . On a bed, the pillow*
*high and light,*
*how the dizziness slipped away*
*like a fish in the sea . . .*

On the two-branched highway
we were leaving, bodies only,
with our hearts on each branch
separate, one right, one left.

# Denial

On the secret sea-shore
white like a pigeon
we thirsted at noon:
but the water was brackish.

On the golden sand
we wrote her name;
but the sea-breeze blew
and the writing vanished.

With what spirit, what heart,
what desire and passion
we lived our life: a mistake!
So we changed our life.

## The Companions in Hades

*fools, who ate the cattle of Helios Hyperion;*
*but he deprived them of the day of their return.*

– ODYSSEY

Since we still had some hardtack
how stupid of us
to go ashore and eat
the Sun's slow cattle,

for each was a castle
you'd have to battle
forty years, till you'd become
a hero and a star!

On the earth's back we hungered,
but when we'd eaten well
we fell to these lower regions
mindless and satisfied.

# Fog

*Say it with a ukulele*

'Say it with a ukulele...'
grumbles some gramophone;
Christ, tell me what to say to her
now that I'm used to my loneliness?

With accordions squeezed
by well-dressed beggars
they call on the angels
and their angels are hell.

And the angels opened their wings
but, below, the mists condensed,
thank God, for otherwise they'd catch
our poor souls like thrushes.

And life's cold as a fish
— Is that how you live? — Yes, how else?
So many are the drowned
down on the sea's bed.

Trees are like corals
their colour gone,
carts are like ships
sunken and lonely...

'Say it with a ukulele...'
Words for words, and more words?
Love, where's your church,
I'm tired of this hermitage.

Ah, were life but straight
how we'd live it then!
But it's fated otherwise,
you have to turn in a small corner.

And what corner is it? Who knows?
Lights shine on lights
pallidly, the hoar-frosts are dumb,
and our soul's in our teeth.

Will we find consolation?
Day put on night –
everything is night, everything is night –
we'll find something, if we search . . .

'Say it with a ukelele . . . '
I see her red nails –
how they must glow in firelight –
and I remember her with her cough.

*London, Christmas 1924*

## The Mood of a Day

*We plainly saw that not a soul*
*lived in that fated vessel!*

— EDGAR ALLAN POE

The mood of a day that we lived ten years ago in a foreign
    country
the airy spirit of an ancient moment that took on wings and
    vanished like an angel of the Lord
the voice of a woman forgotten with such care and such
    pain
an end inconsolable, the marble setting of some September.

New houses dusty clinics exanthematic windows coffin-
    shops . . .
Has anyone considered the suffering of a sensitive
    pharmacist on night duty?
The room in a mess: drawers windows doors open their
    mouths like wild animals;
a tired man lays out the cards, searches, astrologizes,
    scrutinizes.

He worries: if they knock at the door who will open it? If he
    opens a book whom will he look at? If he opens his soul
    who will look? Chain.
Where is love that with one stroke cuts time in two and
    stuns it?
Words only and gestures. A monotonous monologue in
    front of a mirror under a wrinkle.
Like a drop of ink on a handkerchief, the boredom spreads.

Everyone in the ship is dead, but the ship keeps going the
    way it was heading when it put out from the harbour
how the captain's nails grew . . . and the boatswain, who had
    three mistresses in every port, unshaven . . .
The sea swells slowly, the rigging fills with pride, and the
    day is turning mild.
Three dolphins flash black, glistening; the mermaid smiles,
    and a forgotten sailor waves astride the yardarm.

## Rocket

It isn't the sea
it isn't the world
this blue light
on our fingers

under the eyelids
a thousand antennae
grope giddily
to find the sky

red carnation
alone in your vase
as I wrote you stood
before me like love

there was a deer
yellow as sulphur
there was a tower
built of gold

five crows
counted their years
quarrelled and scattered
like a pentacle

lilies whitened
the beloved's hair
on the beloved's body
I wrote whole books.

I can't live
only with peacocks
nor travel always
in the mermaid's eyes.

# Rhyme

Lips, guardians of my love that was to fade
hands, bonds of my youth that was to go
colour of a face lost in nature somewhere
trees . . . birds . . . hunting . . .

Body, black in the sun's heat like a grape
body, my rich ship, where are you travelling?
It's the hour when twilight drowns
and I tire searching the darkness . . .

(Our life shrinks every day).

# EROTIKOS LOGOS

There is a most vain class among men which, despising ordinary things, fixes its eyes on distant things, pursuing empty air with idle hopes...

— PINDAR

# Erotikos Logos

### I

Rose of fate, you looked for ways to wound us
yet you bent like the secret about to be released
and the command you chose to give us was beautiful
and your smile was like a ready sword.

The ascent of your cycle livened creation
from your thorn emerged the way's thought
our impulse dawned naked to possess you
the world was easy: a simple pulsation.

II

The secrets of the sea are forgotten on the shores
the darkness of the depths is forgotten in the surf;
the corals of memory suddenly shine purple . . .
O do not stir . . . listen to hear its light

motion . . . you touched the tree with the apples
the hand reached out, the thread points the way and guides
        you . . .
O dark shivering in the roots and the leaves
if it were but you who would bring the forgotten dawn!

May lilies blossom again on the meadow of separation
may days open mature, the embrace of the heavens,
may those eyes alone shine in the glare
the pure soul be outlined like the song of a flute.

Was it night that shut its eyes? Ashes remain,
as from the string of a bow a choked hum remains,
ash and dizziness on the black shore
and dense fluttering imprisoned in surmise.

Rose of the wind, you knew but took us unknowing
at a time when thought was building bridges
so that fingers would knit and two fates pass by
and spill into the low and rested light.

III

O dark shivering in the roots and the leaves!
Come forth sleepless form in the gathering silence
raise your head from your cupped hands
so that your will be done and you tell me again

the words that touched and merged with the blood like an
      embrace;
and let your desire, deep like the shade of a walnut tree,
      bend
and flood us with your lavish hair
from the down of the kiss to the leaves of the heart.

You lowered your eyes and you had the smile
that masters of another time humbly painted.
Forgotten reading from an ancient gospel,
your words breathed and your voice was gentle:

'The passing of time is soft and unworldly
and pain floats lightly in my soul
dawn breaks in the heavens, the dream remains afloat
and it's as if scented shrubs were passing.

'With my eyes' startling, with my body's blush
a flock of doves awakens and descends
their low, circling flight entangles me
the stars are a human touch on my breast.

'I hear, as in a sea shell, the distant
adverse and confused lament of the world
but these are moments only, they disappear,
and the two-branched thought of my desire reigns alone.

'It seemed I'd risen naked in a vanished recollection
when you came, strange and familiar, my beloved
to grant me, bending, the boundless deliverance
I was seeking from the wind's quick sistrum . . . '

The broken sunset declined and was gone
and it seemed a delusion to ask for the gifts of the sky.
You lowered your eyes. The moon's thorn blossomed
and you became afraid of the mountain's shadows.

*. . . In the mirror how our love diminishes*
*in sleep the dreams, school of oblivion*
*in the depths of time, how the heart contracts*
*and vanishes in the rocking of a foreign embrace . . .*

IV

Two serpents, beautiful, apart, tentacles of separation
crawl and search, in the night of the trees,
for a secret love in hidden bowers;
sleepless they search, they neither drink nor eat.

Circling, twisting, their insatiable intent
spins, multiplies, turns, spreads rings on the body
which the laws of the starry dome silently govern,
stirring its hot, irrepressible frenzy.

The forest stands as a shivering pillar for night
and the silence is a silver cup where moments fall
echoes distinct, whole, a careful chisel
sustained by carved lines . . .

The statue suddenly dawns. But the bodies have vanished
in the sea in the wind in the sun in the rain.
So the beauties nature grants us are born
but who knows if a soul hasn't died in the world.

The parted serpents must have circled in fantasy
(the forest shimmers with birds, shoots, blossoms)
their wavy searching still remains,
like the turnings of the cycle that bring sorrow.

V

Where is the double-edged day that had changed
     everything?
Won't there be a navigable river for us?
Won't there be a sky to drop refreshing dew
for the soul benumbed and nourished by the lotus?

On the stone of patience we wait for the miracle
that opens the heavens and makes all things possible
we wait for the angel as in the age-old drama
at the moment when the open roses of twilight

disappear . . . Red rose of the wind and of fate,
you remained in memory only, a heavy rhythm
rose of the night, you passed, undulating purple
undulation of the sea . . . The world is simple.

*Athens, October '29– December '30*

# The Cistern

*To George Apostolidis*

I found I had to put the hospital of Don Juan Tavera in the form of a model, because not only did it nearly cover the gate of Visagra, but also its dome rose so that it dominated the town; and once I'd put it in to look like a model and had shifted it from its place, it seemed to me preferable to show its façade rather than its other sides. As for its position in the town, that appears on the map.

– DOMENIKOS THEOTOKOPOULOS

# The Cistern

Here, in the earth, a cistern has taken root
den of secret water that gathers there.
Its roof, resounding steps. The stars
don't blend with its heart. Each day
grows, opens and shuts, doesn't touch it.

The world above opens like a fan
and plays with the wind's breath
in a rhythm that expires at sunset
flaps its wings hopelessly and throbs
at the whistling of a destined suffering.

On the curve of the dome of a pitiless night
cares tread, joys move by
with fate's quick rattle
faces light up, shine a moment
and die out in an ebony darkness.

Faces that go! In rows, the eyes
roll in a gutter of bitterness
and the signs of the great day
take them up and bring them closer
to the black earth that asks no ransom.

Man's body bends to earth
so that thirsty love remain;
turned into marble at time's touch,
the statue falls naked on the ripe breast
that softly sweetens it.

The thirst of love looks for tears
the roses bend – our soul;
the pulse of nature sounds on the leaves
dusk approaches like a passer-by
then night, then the grave.

But here in the earth a cistern has taken root
warm, secret den that hoards
the groan of each body in the air
the battle with night, with day
the world grows, passes, does not touch it.

Time goes by, suns and moons,
but the water has hardened like a mirror:
expectation open-eyed
when all the sails sink
at the edge of the sea that nourishes it.

Alone, and in its heart such a crowd
alone, and in its heart such labour
and such pain, drop by drop alone
casting its nets far into a world
that lives with bitter undulation.

When the wave moved out of the embrace
would that it ended in the embrace
would that it gave us love on the shore
before breaking its line
the wave, as it remained foam on the sand.

A warmth stretched out like hide
tame like a sleeping beast
that calmly avoided fear
and knocked on sleep to ask
for the garden where silver drops.

And a body hidden, deep cry
let out from the cave of death
like water lively in the ditch
like water shining on the grass
alone, talking to the black roots . . .

O nearer the root of our life
than our thoughts and our anxiety!
O nearer than our stern brother
who looks at us with eyelids closed,
and nearer than the spear still in our side!

O if the skin of silence now constricting us
would only soften suddenly at our touch
so that we might forget, O gods, the crime
that daily grows and weighs upon us,
so that we might escape the knowledge and the hunger!

Gathering up the pain of our wound
so that we may escape the pain of our wound
gathering up the body's bitterness
so that we may escape the body's bitterness
so that roses may bloom in the blood of our wound.

May everything become as it was at first
to fingers eyes and lips
may we throw off the aged sickness,
skin shed by snakes
yellow in the green clover.

Great and immaculate love, serenity!
In the lively fever one night
you bent humbly, naked curve,
white wing over the flock,
like a light palm on the temple.

The sea that brought you carried you away
to the blossoming lemon trees
now that the fates have woken gently,
a thousand faces with three plain wrinkles,
placed in escort to the epitaph.

The myrrh-bearers drag their dirges
so that man's hope may follow
wedged in the eyes by flames
lighting the blind earth
that sweats from the effort of spring.

Flames of the world beyond, candles
over spring surging forth today,
mournful shadows on dead wreaths
footsteps . . . footsteps . . . the slow bell
unwinds a dark chain.

'We are dying! Our gods are dying!...'
The marble statues know it, looking down
like white dawn upon the victim
alien, full of eyelids, fragments,
as the crowds of death pass by.


. . . . . . . . . .
. . . . . . . . . .
. . . . . . . . . .
. . . . . . . . . .
. . . . . . . . . .


They passed into the distance, their sorrow
hot near the lowered church candles
that inscribed on their bent foreheads
the life full of joy at noon
when magic spells and the stars expire.

But night does not believe in dawn
and love lives to weave death
thus, like a free soul,
a cistern that teaches silence
in the flaming city.

# OTHER RHYMED POEMS

from

*Book of Exercises*
*Logbook II*
*Logbook III*

## Pantoum

The stars contain a world of their own
ships drag fires over the sea
my soul, inflamed and bitter as you pray devoutly,
free yourself from the link of darkness.

Ships drag fires over the sea
night shrinks and stays still as though a stranger
my soul, inflamed and bitter as you pray devoutly,
you recognize the law that binds you.

Night shrinks and stays still as though a stranger
the lights have gone out over the black silk
my soul, you recognize the law that binds you,
and what will stay with you, what abandon you.

The lights have gone out over the black silk
there's no sound but the rattle of time;
what will stay with you, what abandon you
should the dumb loophole explode with a flash.

There's no sound but the rattle of time
metallic column at the limit of pain
should the dumb loophole explode with a flash
you won't find even a dream to shed a tear.

Metallic column at the limit of pain
the moment rises like a suspended blade
you won't find even a dream to shed a tear
among your immaterial throng that constricts like a snake.

The moment rises like a suspended blade
why does peace delay its coming?
Among your immaterial throng that constricts like a snake
there's no heaven nor angelic happiness.

Why does peace delay its coming?
Among the taciturn counting their sorrow
there's no heaven nor angelic happiness:
the stars contain a world of their own.

# Crickets

The house is full of crickets
beating like rhythmless clocks
out of breath. And the times

we live beat that way too
while the just remain silent
as though they had nothing to say.

Once in Pelion I heard them
swiftly digging a cave
in the night. But now

we've flipped the leaf of fate
and you've known us as we've known you
from those who live in the north

to the negroes at the equator
all body without mind
who bellow when in pain.

I suffer and you suffer
but we don't yell or cry
or whisper even, because

the machine is very quick
at horror and contempt
at death and life.

The house is full of crickets.

*Pretoria, 16 January '42*

## Actors, Middle East

We put up theatres and tear them down
wherever we happen to find ourselves
we put up theatres and set the stage
but our fate always triumphs in the end

and sweeps them away as it sweeps us too
actors and the actors' manager
prompter and musicians all disappear
scattered to the five hungry winds.

Bodies, mats, wood, make-up
rhymes, feelings, veils, jewellery
masks, sunsets, wails and howls
exclamations and suns rising

cast off helter-skelter along with us
(where are we going? where are you going?)
nerves naked upon our skin
like the stripes of an onager or zebra

exposed and naked, dry and burning
(when were we born? when buried?)
and taut like the strings of a lyre
incessantly humming. Look also

at our heart: a sponge
ambling through the street and market-place
soaking up the blood and bile
of both the tetrarch and the thief.

*Middle East, August '43*

# Agianapa II

*Spring 1156*

*Verses for music*

Under the ageing sycamore
madly the wind was playing
with the birds with the branches
but it never spoke to us.

Welcome and good luck O breath of the soul
we opened our hearts to you
do come in, do drink in
your fill of our desire.

Under the ageing sycamore
the wind rose up and left,
gone to the northern castles,
and never touched us even.

O my rosemary, O my thyme,
bind your breast tightly
and find a cave, find a lair
and hide away your light.

This is no Palm Sunday wind
no wind of the Resurrection
but a wind of fire, a wind of smoke,
a wind of joyless life.

Under the ageing sycamore
the wind returned dry,
reeking of florins everywhere,
and bartered us for gold.

## In the Kyrenia District

> *But I'm dying and done for*
> *What on earth was all the fun for?*
> *For God's sake keep that sunlight out of sight.*
>
> —JOHN BETJEMAN
>
> *Homer's world, not ours.*
>
> — W. H. AUDEN

*Sketch for an 'idyll'*

.  .  .  .  .  .  .  .  .  .  .  .  .  .  .

– I wired her flowers.
                              – Whisky? Gin?
– Today's her silver wedding.
                                        – Mind the dog
  doesn't jump up against your skirt:
  he'll muddy it. They neglect him, he's getting too
      familiar.
– Gin, please. She lives in Kent now. I'll
  always remember her in the church. When we came out,
      it was raining; a band
  was playing on the pavement opposite, the Salvation
      Army, I think.
– Sometime in May, the year of the General Strike.
– We didn't even have newspapers.
                                        – Look at the mountain:
  when the sun finally sets it'll be one colour all over,
      and peaceful.
  That's St Hilarion. I prefer it by moonlight.
– She writes that it has a ghost who goes about with an
      extinguished lamp.
– St Hilarion?
                    – No, her house in Kent.
– The ghost would be more appropriate here. Sometimes –
  I can't explain it – memory

grows harsher in this light, dough
dried by the sun . . .
                              – What kind of dough?
I get headaches too.
                              – Did you meet the poet,
or whatever he was, staying here last month?
He called feeling palimpsestic libido;
most unusual; no one knows
what he means. A cynic and philhellene.
– An introverted snob.
                              – Amusing sometimes. Now he's taking the baths.
– In Italy I heard.
                              – Yes, some 'spa'.
He says it encourages sexual vigour.
I gave him an introduction to Horace in Rome.
– How could you, he's so shocking.
                                        – How, indeed?
Maybe at our age one makes allowances
maybe out of need to escape from my ordinary self
maybe it's this island that bores me like a meteor from
        another world.
– You're becoming sad, Margaret. But it's so beautiful:
the sun, the sea, an everlasting summer.
                                        – Ah, this view
that questions and questions. Have you ever noticed how
        the mirror sometimes
makes our faces death-like? Or how that thief the sun
takes our make-up off each morning? I'd prefer
the sun's warmth without the sun; I'd look for
a sea that doesn't strip one bare: a voiceless blue
without that ill-bred daily interrogation.
The silent caress of the mist in the tassels of dream
        would refresh me:
this world isn't ours, it's Homer's –

that's the best description I've heard of this place.
Quiet, Rex!
                    – No, please don't bother,
I know the way. I'd like to have time to buy some cloth:
thirty yards of woven stuff, for our gardener Panagi;
incredible, he says he needs that much for those old
      baggy trousers he wears...
As you were speaking I remembered Bill, one Saturday,
on the Thames... I gazed at his scarf all evening long.
As he rowed he was whistling, 'Say it with a ukulele'.
What's become of him, I wonder?
                                   – He was killed in Crete.
– He was handsome, so handsome... I'll expect you on
      Tuesday...
How softly the Thames flowed among the shadows...
      Sleep well.
– It's a pity you can't stay for dinner.

# Pedlar from Sidon

*At once you knew him for the son of a*
*full-breasted Aphrodite and of Hermes.*

— Christodoros's *Description*

The young pedlar came from Sidon
without being afraid of angry Poseidon.
His curls crow-coloured, his chiton purple,
fastened at the shoulder by a golden clasp,
his body reeking of myrrh and make-up.
He entered Cyprus through Famagusta,
now enjoys the sunlight
of back lanes in Nicosia.
In the courtyard a young Turkish girl:
the creeper that she trims with ivory fingers
sways shyly to her touch.
The pedlar crosses the sun's river
like a walking god, the song he sings
dream-soft: 'Roses in a kerchief . . . ',
as if his crimson lips
longed to kiss Zeus's sandals.
He walks on so, then stops
to sit beside a Gothic gatepost
that offers the wild-eyed lion of Mark
glaring down on a sleeping goatherd
who smells too much of goat and sweat.
The pedlar leans back; his hand
feels inside his shirt, removes
a terracotta statuette.
He studies it: a naked youth that glides,
uncertain, on the effeminate couch
between concave Hermes and convex Aphrodite.

# BIBLIOGRAPHICAL NOTE

IN THIS NOTE we do not attempt to cite all possible sources that would be relevant to a thorough study of Seferis's poetry. We offer here only a list that includes the first Greek editions of the various volumes that constitute Seferis's collected poems, the definitive collected edition of his work in Greek, his principal prose works, the latest editions of his principal translations, selected translations of his work into English, and a bibliography.

## I. FIRST EDITIONS OF SEFERIS'S POEMS
### (published as volumes)

*Στροφή* [Turning Point], Athens, 1931.

*Ἡ Στέρνα* [The Cistern], Athens, 1932.

*Μυθιστόρημα* [Mythistorema], Athens, 1935.

*Γυμνοπαιδία* [Gymnopaidia], Athens, 1936.

*Τετράδιο Γυμνασμάτων* [Book of Exercises], Athens, 1940.

*Ἡμερολόγιο Καταστρώματος* [Logbook I], Athens, 1940.

*Ἡμερολόγιο Καταστρώματος, Β'* [Logbook II], Alexandria, 1944.

*«Κίχλη»* ['Thrush'], Athens, 1947.

*Ἡμερολόγιο Καταστρώματος, Γ'* [Logbook III], Athens, 1955 (originally published as ... *Κύπρον, οὗ μ'ἐθέσπισεν*...).

*Τρία Κρυφά Ποιήματα* [Three Secret Poems], Athens, 1966.

*Ποιήματα μέ ζωγραφιές γιά μικρά παιδιά* [Poems with Paintings for Young Children], Athens, 1975.

*Τετράδιο Γυμνασμάτων, Β'* [Book of Exercises II], Athens, 1976. Ἐπιμέλεια Γ. Π. Σαββίδης.

## II. COLLECTED EDITION OF SEFERIS'S POEMS

*Ποιήματα* [Poems], ἔνατη ἔκδοση, Athens, 1974. Ἐπιμέλεια Γ. Π. Σαββίδης. [All subsequent 'editions' are reprints of this ninth edition.]

III. SEFERIS'S PRINCIPAL PROSE WORKS

*Τρείς μέρες στά μοναστήρια τής Καππαδοκίας* [Three Days at the Monasteries of Kappadokia], Athens, 1953. Also in French: Institut Français, Athens, 1953.

*Χειρόγραφο Σεπ. '41* [Manuscript Sept. '41], Athens, 1972.

*Ἰγνάτης Τρελός / Γιῶργος Σεφέρης: Οἱ ὧρες τής «Κυρίας Ἔρσης»* [The Hours of 'Madame Ersi'], Athens, 1973.

*Μέρες τοῦ 1945–1951* [Days of 1945–1951], Athens, 1973.

*Ἔξη νύχτες στήν Ἀκρόπολη* [Six Nights on the Acropolis], Athens, 1974. Ἐπιμέλεια Γ. Π. Σαββίδης.

*Δοκιμές* [Essays], δ' ἔκδοση, Τόμος Α' καὶ Β', Athens, 1981. Ἐπιμέλεια Γ. Π. Σαββίδης.

*Μέρες Α': 16 Φεβρουαρίου 1925–17 Αὐγούστου 1931* [Days I: 16 February 1925–17 August 1931], Athens, 1975.

*Μέρες Β': 24 Αὐγούστου 1931–12 Φεβρουαρίου 1934* [Days II: 24 August 1931–12 February 1934], Athens, 1975.

*Μέρες Γ': 16 Ἀπρίλη 1934–14 Δεκέμβρη 1940* [Days III: 16 April 1934–14 December 1940], Athens, 1977.

*Πολιτικὸ Ἡμερολόγιο Α': 25 Νοέμβρη 1935–13 Ὀκτώβρη 1944* [Political Journal I: 25 November 1935–13 October 1944], Athens, 1979. Ἐπιμέλεια Ἀλέξ. Ξύδη.

*Πολιτικὸ Ἡμερολόγιο Β': 1945–1947, 1949, 1952* [Political Journal II: 1945–1947, 1949, 1952], Athens, 1985. Ἐπιμέλεια Ἀλέξ. Ξύδη.

*Μέρες Δ': 1 Φενάρη 1941–31 Δεκέμβρη 1944* [Days IV: 1 January 1941–31 December 1944], β' ἔκδοση, Athens, 1986.

*Μέρες Ε': 1 Γενάρη 1945–19 Ἀπρίλη 1951* [Days V: 1 January 1945–19 April 1951], Athens, 1986. Ἐπιμέλεια Ἐ. Χ. Κάσδαγλη. Reprint of *Μέρες τοῦ 1945–1951* [Days of 1945–1951], Athens, 1973.

*Μέρες Στ': 20 Ἀπρίλη 1951–4 Αὐγούστου 1956* [Days VI: 20 April 1951–4 August 1956], Athens, 1986. Ἐπιμέλεια Παν. Μέρμηγκα.

*Χειρόγραφο Ὀκτ. '68* [Manuscript Oct. '68], Εἰσαγωγὴ-Σημειώσεις Π. Ἀ. Ζάννα, Athens, 1986.

*Μέρες Ζ': 1 Ὀκτώβρη 1956–27 Δεκέμβρη 1960* [Days VII: 1 October 1956–27 December 1960], Ἐπιμέλεια Θεανώς Μιχαηλίδου, Athens, 1990.

IV. SEFERIS'S PRINCIPAL TRANSLATIONS (latest editions)

*Άσμα ἀσμάτων*, ὁριστική ἔκδοση, Athens, 1972.

Θ. Σ. "Ελιοτ, *Ἡ "Ερημη Χώρα καὶ ἄλλα ποιήματα*, Athens, 1986.

Θ. Σ. "Ελιοτ, *Φονικό στήν 'Εκκλησιά*, ὁριστική ἔκδοση, Athens, 1974.

*Ἡ 'Αποκάλυψη τού 'Ιωάννη*, ὁριστική ἔκδοση, Athens, 1975.

*'Αντιγραφές*, ὁριστική ἔκδοση, Athens, 1978. 'Επιμέλεια Γ. Π. Σαββίδης.

*Μεταγραφές*, 'Επιμέλεια Γ. Γιατρομανολάκη, Athens, 1980.

V. SELECTED TRANSLATIONS OF SEFERIS INTO ENGLISH

Bernard Spencer, Nanos Valaoritis, Lawrence Durrell: *The King of Asine and Other Poems*, London, 1948. Introduction by Rex Warner.

Edmund Keeley and Philip Sherrard: *Six Poets of Modern Greece*, London, 1960 and New York, 1961. Introduction and Notes by the translators. Includes a selection of Seferis.

Rex Warner: *Poems*, London, 1960 and Boston, 1981. Introduction and Notes by the translator.

Philip Sherrard: *Delphi*, Munich and Ahrbeck, Hanover, 1963.

Rex Warner and Th. D. Frangopoulos: *On the Greek Style*, Boston, 1966 and Athens, 1982. Selected essays from *Δοκιμές*. Reprint: Athens, 1982.

Walter Kaiser: *Three Secret Poems*, Cambridge, Mass., 1969.

Peter Thompson: 'Three Private Poems', *Agenda* Vol. 7 No. 1, Winter 1969, pp. 35–49.

Kimon Friar: *Modern Greek Poetry*, New York, 1973. Introduction and Notes by the translator. Includes a selection of Seferis.

Athan Anagnostopoulos: *A Poet's Journal: Days of 1945–1951*, Cambridge, Mass., 1974.

Edmund Keeley and Philip Sherrard: *The Dark Crystal*, Athens, 1980, reprinted as *A Greek Quintet*, Limni, Greece, 1992. American edition: *Voices of Modern Greece*, Princeton, 1981. Preface and Notes by the translators. Includes a selection of Seferis.

VI.   BIBLIOGRAPHY

Δημήτρης Δασκαλόπουλος: *Ἐργογραφία Σεφέρη, (1931–1979), Βιβλιογραφική δοκιμή*. Ἑλληνικό Λογοτεχνικό καὶ Ἱστορικό Ἀρχεῖο, Athens, 1979. Supplement: 'Βιβλιογραφία Σεφέρη (1979–1986)', *Διαβάζω, ἀρ. 142*, 23 April 1986, pp. 138–147.

# NOTES

THE FOLLOWING notes are intended to be factual rather than interpretive. Some derive from Seferis's own notes to the sixth edition of his Ποιήματα (Athens, 1965). A few are based upon George Savidis's notes to subsequent editions of Seferis published by Ikaros, Athens. The additional notes are included to assist the English-speaking reader generally, as well as the specialist in modern Greek literature.

Page

1    *Mythistorema*: the colloquial meaning of the title is 'novel', but it has other connotations also, as the poet indicates in the following note: 'MYTHISTOREMA – it is its two components that made me choose the title of this work: MYTHOS, because I have used, clearly enough, a certain mythology; ISTORIA (both 'history' and 'story'), because I have tried to express, with some coherence, circumstances that are as independent from myself as the characters in a novel.'

1    Epigraph: Rimbaud, 'Fêtes de la Faim', lines 3–4. 'If I have any *taste*, it is scarcely for anything but earth and stones.'

4    *The poet* referred to is Dionysios Solomos, and the phrase cited is from his prose work, *The Woman of Zakynthos*, Chapter I.

5    Epigraph: Aeschylus, *The Libation Bearers*, 491. Orestes is speaking at Agamemnon's tomb, reminding his father of the bath where he was slain by Clytemnestra.

6    Lines 1–4: the quotation is from Plato, *Alcibiades*, 133B. In a note on the poem, Seferis says that these words, spoken by Socrates to Alcibiades, once gave him a sensation akin to that evoked by the following lines from Baudelaire's 'La Mort des amants':

> Nos deux cœurs seront deux vastes flambeaux,
> Qui réfléchiront leurs doubles lumières
> Dans nos deux esprits, ces miroirs jumeaux.

7    *Their oars/mark the place...*: see Homer, *Odyssey*, XI.75 ff., where the shade of Elpenor, youngest of Odysseus's companions, asks that his oar be planted on his sea-shore grave to perpetuate his memory. See also the note to p. 145 on Elpenor.

9   *M. R.*: the initials are those of Maurice Ravel (1875–1937), the
    French composer.

13   *Asphodels*: in Homeric mythology the meadow of asphodels is
     the dwelling-place of the dead. See *Odyssey*, XI and XXIV.12
     ff.

14   *Cool coronals and the fingers*: during the wedding ceremony in
     the Orthodox Church, the bridal pair exchange both crowns
     and rings.

14   The *Symplegades*, through which Jason and the Argonauts had
     to pass, were dangerous clashing rocks at the juncture of the
     Bosphorus and the Black Sea (Pontus Euxinus).

16   *The youngest . . .* : see note to p. 7.

17   *Hydra*, a rock island off the north-eastern coast of the Pelopon-
     nese, contributed substantially to the naval forces that helped to
     win independence for Greece in the early nineteenth century.
     This contribution is celebrated annually with colourful festivi-
     ties.

19   Epigraph: Pliny, *Letters*, I.3. 'And what about that shadiest of
     plane trees?'

20   Epigraph: Sophocles, *Electra*, 694. From the passage which
     describes Orestes's participation in the chariot-races at Delphi.

21   *Astyanax*: younger son of Hector and Andromache. At the fall
     of Troy he was either flung from the walls by Neoptolemus or
     killed by Odysseus. See also the *Iliad*, VI.402–3.

24   *The sea, the sea . . .* : Aeschylus, *Agamemnon*, 958. The line is
     from the speech by Clytemnestra justifying Agamemnon's
     treading on the purple carpet leading into the palace.

28   *Erebus*: see *Odyssey*, X.526 ff. where Odysseus is instructed by
     Circe to sacrifice, on visiting the dead, a young lamb and a
     black ewe, turning their heads towards Erebus.

35   In a note to the first edition of *Book of Exercises*, Seferis writes:
     'This book is made up either of various poems which have no
     place in any of the other selections that I've already published
     or might publish later, or of occasional pieces dedicated to
     friends, or of exercises, some more complete in form than
     others. Under the circumstances, the book has, I imagine, no
     other coherence than that provided by ten years of continuous
     effort towards poetic expression, and perhaps it is nothing
     more than a contribution to criticism.'

39  *Kifisia* is a relatively cool, well-watered, now densely popu-
lated residential district lying some eight miles north of central
Athens.

39  *Aidipsos*, on the north-west coast of Euboea, has been a famous
spa since Roman times.

41  *George Theotokas* (1905–1966) wrote a number of novels and
plays, including *Argo*, a novel translated into English and
published in London by Methuen and Co. Ltd. in 1951. Theo-
tokas 'discovered' Syngrou Avenue in his early work, *'Ελεύ-
θερο Πνεύμα* [Free Spirit], published in 1929. The avenue,
running from the Temple of Olympian Zeus to Faleron and the
sea, was at that time the broadest in Athens, 'one of the sym-
bols of the new era which it was our destiny to express',
according to Theotokas (in *'Εποχές*, Athens, February 1964, p.
14). In *'Ελεύθερο Πνεύμα* he writes: 'Day and night, towards
the Faleron shore, Syngrou Avenue carries the newly born and
still unexpressed rhythms of a powerful lyricism that call for
powerful poets.' Cf. the second stanza of 'A Word for Sum-
mer', p. 89.

42  Line 1: cf. Joachim du Bellay, 'Heureux qui, comme Ulysse, a
fait un beau voyage' (*Les Regrets*).

43  The *Erotokritos* is a Cretan epic of the seventeenth century
written by Vitzentzos Kornaros, a work of 10,052 verses in the
chivalrous genre, telling of the love of Aretousa, the daughter
of a king, and the valiant Erotokritos. Seferis has written a
critical study of this work, reprinted in *Δοκιμές* (Athens, 1974).

44  Epigraph: Book III, I.10 of his *Meditations*. 'This brief
thing...'

50  *Symplegades*: see note to p. 14.

51  *D. I. Antoniou* (b. 1906), a contemporary Greek poet (see
Keeley and Sherrard, *Six Poets of Modern Greece*, London,
1960), served for a number of years as an officer in the Greek
merchant marine. The title of the poem is a nautical term
identifying the direction of the prevailing wind: between Si-
rocco and Levante, or ESE.

52  *Pelion* is a mountain range in Thessalian Magnesia. The cen-
taur, Chiron, is said to have dwelt on its wooded slopes.

52  *Santorini*: see the epigraph to *Gymnopaidia*, p. 29.

52  *Spetses, Poros* and *Mykonos* are popular Aegean islands.

52  *Omonia* ('harmony') and *Syntagma* ('constitution') are the two
largest squares in central Athens. The dialogue here makes use
of *katharevousa*, the purist language, to suggest a touch of
affectation in the speakers.

53  *The Aegean flower with corpses:* Aeschylus, *Agamemnon*, 659.

57  *Stratis Thalassinos:* literally 'Stratis the Mariner', a persona that
appears frequently in Seferis's poetry.

62  Line 3: Aeschylus, *Eumenides*, 143. The cries are uttered by the
Furies after they have been aroused from their sleep in the
temple of Apollo at Delphi by Clytemnestra's ghost and urged
to continue their task of hunting down Orestes.

63  *Fires of St John:* on the eve of the feast-day of St John (24 June),
it was customary in Seferis's childhood village of Skala near the
town of Vourla in Asia Minor – as in other Greek communities
generally – for the children to light small fires in the streets after
sunset and jump over them for good luck (see Nikos E. Milio-
ris, *Τά Βούρλα τῆς Μικρᾶς 'Ασίας*, Athens, 1965, II, 236).
Among the various divinatory rituals practised by unmarried
girls on this feast-day are the two mentioned in the poem: *a*)
The girl drops molten lead into a container filled with 'silent'
water (i.e. water brought secretly from a spring by a young
girl or boy who is forbidden to speak to anyone on the way),
and the shape that the lead takes on cooling indicates the trade
or profession that the girl's future husband will follow; *b*) The
girl undresses at midnight and stands naked before a mirror,
invoking St John and asking him to reveal the man she will
marry; the first name that she hears on waking the next morn-
ing is that of her future husband (see G. A. Megas, *'Ελληνικαί
'Εορταί καί 'Εθιμα τῆς Λαϊκῆς Λατρείας*, Athens, 1963, pp.
217–8).

63  *Herostratus:* in 356 B.C. Herostratus burned down the famous
Temple of Artemis at Ephesus in order to make his name
immortal.

65  *Nijinsky:* the famous Russian dancer.

76  *Enough of life:* Aeschylus, *Agamemnon*, 1,314; from Cassandra's
speech just before she enters the palace to be murdered.

76  *And yet there is the sea . . . :* Aeschylus, *Agamemnon*, 958. See
note to p. 24.

77   *Don Juan Tavera*: see the epigraph to *The Cistern*, p. 253, and the note to it.

79   Epigraph: 'at the white watches'.

89   *Syngrou Avenue*: see note to p. 41.

103   Epigraph: 'Bread and Wine' part 7, lines 11–14.

107   *Ghegs* and *Tosks* are the names of two Albanian tribes.

108   *Vercingetorix* was the son of a former king of the Gallic tribe, the Averni. He led the Gallic revolt against Caesar in 52 B.C., was defeated and put to death after Caesar's triumph.

108   *Tel qu'en lui-même...*: Stéphane Mallarmé, 'Le Tombeau d'Edgar Poe', line 1.

109   Line 1: the opening line of Marcel Proust's *À la recherche du temps perdu (Du côté de chez Swann)*.

109   *Hylas* was a page and companion of Heracles and the Argonauts.

115   *The Container of the Uncontainable*: in Greek, Ἡ Χώρα τού Ἀχωρήτου. This is one of the epithets applied to the Virgin as the Mother of the infinite, and therefore uncontainable, Deity. From it derives the name of the Church of the Saviour of the Chora (Kariye Camii) at Constantinople.

121   *And our women slaves...*: the allusion is to the *Iliad*, VI.457: 'Then in Argos... you shall bear water from Messeïs or Hypereia' (the line is from Hector's speech to Andromache); and also to Thucydides, VII.87: 'At first the Syracusans treated them terribly in the stone quarries...'. The relevant passage refers to the Athenians and their allies who were taken prisoner by the Syracusans after the destruction of the Athenian expedition to Sicily in 413 B.C.

129   Epigraph: Balzac's *Louis Lambert*.

132   Epigraph: *Mythistorema*, 7.

134   Epigraph: *Iliad* II.560; from the catalogue of ships.

134   *The citadel* is the ruined acropolis of Asini, close to the modern village of Tolos on the coast of the Argolid. The landscape has changed considerably since the poem was written.

139   *Gate of the Sun*: one of two large gates of early Alexandria, Egypt, known as the Rosetta Gate in Arabic times. The other was called the Gate of the Moon.

144   *Agapanthi* (literally 'love flowers') are African lilies. For 'Stratis Thalassinos', see note to p. 57.

144   *The region of dreams*: see *Odyssey*, XXIV.12 ff.

144   *The pouch of the winds*: see *Odyssey*, X.19 ff.

145   *Elpenor*, to whom reference has been made in *Mythistorema* (nos. 4 and 12), is a central figure in Seferis's poetry. In Homer's *Odyssey* he is described as a somewhat foolish and feeble-hearted companion who finally kills himself in a fall from Circe's palace while heavy with sleep and wine. Seferis has written of this figure as follows: 'Perhaps you will ask why I write about them [the Elpenor-types] with sympathy. Because the men who belong to this category, among the heroes (in the Homeric sense, not, for God's sake, in the Carlylian) are the most sympathetic. Even the Homeric Odysseus, when he sees Elpenor, first among the dead, pities him and sheds tears. I do not say lovable or admirable, I say sympathetic, sentimental, mediocre, wasted.... He [Elpenor] symbolizes those to whom we refer in daily conversation with the expression: "the poor devil". However, let us not forget that these guileless men, exactly because they are "easy", are often the best carriers of an evil which has its source elsewhere' (see Foreword, fn. 5: same source, p. 502).

145   *On the blackened ridge of Psara*: this line is from Solomos's 'The Destruction of Psara' (1825). The island of Psara was razed and its people massacred during the Greek War of Independence (1821–29). The complete poem, among the more famous in modern Greece, may be rendered as follows:

> On the blackened ridge of Psara
> Glory walking alone
> Recalls the gallant young men:
> On her head she wears a crown
> Made of what little grass
> Remained on that desolate earth.

148   *Stratis Thalassinos*: see note to p. 57.

154   *Now that I sit here, idle...*: the phrase is from the Introduction to the *Memoirs* of General Makriyannis, one of the principal leaders of the Greek War of Independence. His *Memoirs* is, perhaps, the most important prose work in Greek literature of the nineteenth century. See *The Memoirs of General Makriyannis 1797–1864*, ed. and trans. H. A. Lidderdale (London, 1966).

154 *Friendly silences of the moon*: Vergil, *Aeneid*, II.255, 'amica silentia lunae'.

155 *Bad habits, fraud and deceit*: Makriyannis, *Memoirs*, II.258.

156 *Agapanthi*: African lilies. See note to 'Stratis Thalassinos Among the Agapanthi', p. 144.

157 *Drips by day drips in sleep*: cf. Aeschylus, *Agamemnon*, 179–80.

159 *Thrush* was the name of a naval transport sunk off the island of Poros during the Second World War; see Section III of the poem, p. 167.

159 Epigraph: Plutarch, *Consolatio ad Apollonium*, 115D.

161 *The house near the sea*: this house, at the sea's edge on the island of Poros, for a while a hotel, was called 'Γαλήνη' (Serenity). In his 'A Letter on "*Thrush*"' (see Foreword, fn. 5: same source, p. 501), Seferis says: '. . . that Victorian house in Pompeian red gave me, for the first time in many years [i.e. the autumn of 1946], the feeling of a solid building rather than of a temporary tent.'

162 *Elpenor* (see note to p. 145) appears at this point, followed by Circe; they become the protagonists of Section II of the poem.

166 *Soulmonger*: the term was suggested to the poet by the *Agamemnon*, 438: 'Ares, the bodymonger'.

167 *Other voices followed*: see *Odyssey*, XI, *passim*. The voices referred to in this passage are those of the dead in Hades. The *old man* of line 18 is not Teiresias, however, but Socrates, as is indicated by lines 21 ff., which are based on the *Apology* (cf. XXVII, and Socrates's concluding statement).

167 *To drink a drop of blood*: cf. *Odyssey*, XI, *passim*.

169 The *old suppliant* mentioned here is Oedipus; the *invisible fields* are those referred to in Sophocles's *Oedipus at Colonus*, 1,681.

169 *The heart of the Scorpion*: the allusion is to the star Antares of the constellation Scorpio: *cor Scorpionis*.

169 *The daughters of the sea*: see Hesiod, *Theogony*, 270 ff. The *Nereids*, daughters of Nereus and Doris, were nymphs living at the bottom of the sea, reputedly propitious to sailors – especially to the Argonauts. The *Graeae*, children of Phorcys and Ceto, were also reputed to be sea-nymphs: divinities of the white foam seen on waves, grey-haired from birth. The *rising goddess* of the following verse is, of course, Aphrodite.

169 *Whoever has never loved will love*: the line recalls the refrain of the *Pervigilium Veneris*: 'cras amet qui numquam amauit, quique

amauit cras amet.'

169    *Not knowing from where to look out first* . . . : as in the *Erotokritos*, Book I, 1,365.

171    With the exception of 'Memory I' and 'Memory II', the poems in *Logbook III* were written in Cyprus during the poet's visit there in the autumn of 1953. See the poet's note to the first edition.

171    Epigraph: the quotation is from Euripides's *Helen*, where Teucer speaks of 'sea-girt Cyprus, where it was decreed by Apollo that I should live, giving the city the name of Salamis in memory of my island home' (lines 148–50). The quotation appears again in the epigraph to 'Helen', p. 177.

173    *Agianapa* (sometimes spelled Agia Napa) is a village near the sea to the south of Famagusta, Cyprus.

175    *Decorating the gourd*: in a note, the poet says: 'Gourds which are used as jugs. The decoration of these gourds is among the more interesting folk arts of Cyprus: ornamental designs, figures of heroes, either actual or satirical. Only old men were able to give me information about this dying art.' In this instance, the ornamental figures are representations of the damned as they appear in church frescoes of the Second Coming.

175    *Alakátin* is the colloquial term for the well-wheel mentioned here.

176    *In the goddess's name* . . . : see Herodotus, I.199: 'When a woman has once taken her place there, she does not go home before some stranger has thrown money into her lap and has had intercourse with her outside the temple; but as he throws the money, he must say: "I summon you in the name of the goddess Mylitta" (that is, the Assyrian name for Aphrodite). . . . There is a custom like this in some parts of Cyprus.'

177    Euripides's play assumes that not Helen herself but a phantom of Helen went with Paris to Troy. Helen herself was carried by Hermes to the Egyptian court of Proteus, where she was eventually reunited with her husband Menelaus long after the end of the Trojan War.

177    *Platres* is a summer resort on the slopes of Mt Troödos in Cyprus.

178    *The jaws of the sea* . . . : the phrase is taken from a fresco in a countryside church at Asinou in Cyprus.

180   Epigraph: *Revelations*, XXI.1.
182   Epigraph: Dante's *Paradiso*, XIX.146–7. The allusion is to
      Henri II de Lusignan, king of Cyprus and Jerusalem from 1285
      to 1324, regarded by Dante as one of the more lawless and
      perverse monarchs of Christendom. The poem has to do with
      Pierre I de Lusignan, king of Cyprus and Jerusalem from 1359
      to 1369. The relevant historical background can be found in
      R. M. Dawkins's translation and edition of Leontios Makh-
      airas's *Recital concerning the Sweet Land of Cyprus entitled 'Chroni-
      cle'* (Oxford, 1932), I, 215–69 (paras. 234–81).
184   A *Turkopolier* was the commander of the 'Turkopoles' (literally
      'descendants of the Turks'), indigenous troops of Turkish or
      Arabic origin employed by the crusaders as light cavalry. The
      Turkopolier was always a Frank.
185   Epigraph: the translation is by R. M. Dawkins, *op. cit.* I, 445.
      This work is in large part the source for the various historical
      allusions that appear in the poem.
186   *The hangman there in Koutsovendi*: see Dawkins, *op. cit.* I, 595 ff.
      (paras. 599–611). The specific reference is as follows: 'And
      after he was crowned, King James sent to the castle [of Buffa-
      neto near the village of Koutsovendi] and they cut off their
      heads [i.e. of Perot and Wilmot Montolif]; they put them into a
      chest and set them on a mule, and brought them to Cava: and
      the mule died, and there they buried them.'
187   The *Bacchae* were women inspired to ecstatic frenzy by Diony-
      sus. It was concerning them that Euripides wrote his play of
      that title.
188   *Hades and Dionysus are the same*: see Herakleitos: Diels, *Die
      Fragmente der Vorsokratiker*, B 15.
190   Epigraph: Aeschylus, *The Persians*, 894–6. The lines are spo-
      ken by the chorus as they recall the extent and power of the
      Persian Empire under Darius and lament the disaster inflicted
      by the Persian defeat at the battle of Salamis.
190   *The Lord upon many waters*: from Psalm XXVIII (Septuagint).
191   *There is an island*: Aeschylus, *The Persians*, 447. From a speech
      in which the Messenger describes the destruction of the Persian
      fleet at Salamis.
191   *Lord, help us to keep in mind ...*: in a note the poet refers to the
      wartime prayer of Commander Lord Hugh Beresford, R N,

who fell in the battle of Crete: 'O God our loving Father...
Help us to keep in mind the real causes of war: dishonesty,
greed, selfishness, and lack of love, and to drive them out of
this ship, so that she may be a pattern of the new world for
which we are fighting...'

193 *Euripides* is said to have been killed by hunting dogs while
staying at the court of Archelaus, king of Macedonia.

194 *Engomi* is a village to the north-west of Famagusta, Cyprus.

194 *Suddenly I was walking and did not walk... transfixed with his staff
poised*: compare lines 21–37 of this poem with the following
passage, relating to the Virgin's birth of Christ, in 'The Book
of James, or Protevangelium', XVIII.2, of *The Apocryphal
New Testament*, trans. Montague Rhodes James:

> Now I Joseph was walking, and walked not. And I looked
> up to the air and saw the air in amazement. And I looked up
> unto the pole of the heaven and saw it standing still, and the
> fowls of the heaven without motion. And I looked upon the
> earth and saw a dish set, and workmen lying *by it* and their
> hands were in the dish: and they that were chewing chewed
> not, and they that were lifting *the food* lifted not, and they
> that put it to their mouth put it not thereto, but the faces of
> all of them were looking upward. And behold there were
> sheep being driven, and they went not forward but stood
> still; and the shepherd lifted his hand to smite them with his
> staff, and his hand remained up. And I looked upon the
> stream of the river and saw the mouths of the kids upon *the
> water* and they drank not. And of a sudden all things moved
> onward in their course.

199 *Grey-haired sea-nymphs*: the allusion is to the Graeae (see note to
p. 169).

201 *The thunderbolt rules it*: cf. Herakleitos, 'All things are ruled by
the thunderbolt.'

203 *Hecate* was moon goddess of dark forces and magic. She was
often represented in sculpture as a woman with three bodies or
three heads.

204 *The Old Sea-god*: the allusion is to Proteus, called 'The Old
Man of the Sea' by Homer, always changing shape in order to
avoid uttering his unerring prophecies. He appears elsewhere
in Seferis, e.g. pages 50, 139, 155 and 178.

207   *To make the bull-calf mount her*: see Dante, *Purgatorio*, XXVI.41–2.

209   *For things beyond this . . . dig in this same place*: cf. Marcus Aurelius, *Meditations*, Book VII, I.59.

213   *The lead melted for divination*: the ritual alluded to here is among those performed on the eve of the feast-day of St John (24 June). See note to p. 63.

217   *Rex Warner* (1905–1986) was among Seferis's translators. Born in Birmingham, he was a distinguished classicist, translator of classical Greek texts, and novelist (among his novels is *The Wild Goose Chase* [1937], alluded to in line 2).

217   Lines 6–8: the allusion here is to the concluding section of Seferis's '*Thrush*'.

218   *Philetaerus Socius*: in a note to the first edition of the poem, the poet tells us that 'the lines following the reference to "Philetaerus Socius" recall impressions from various exhibits in New York during 1965, e.g. the Museum of Natural History, *Guernica*, etc. The sculptor mentioned is of course Alberto Giacometti; see his letter to Pierre Matisse, 1947: *a*) " . . . j'avais acquis la conviction que le ciel n'est bleu que par convention mais rouge en réalité . . . " and *b*) "Une grande figure était pour moi fausse et une petite tout de même intolérable et puis elles devenaient si minuscules que souvent avec un dernier coup de canif elles disparaissaient dans la poussière" (see *Alberto Giacometti*, ed. Museum of Modern Art, New York, 1965).'

218   The prophet Jonah . . . Nineveh: see *Jonah*, IV.

220   *The Cats of St Nicholas*: see, among other travellers between 1483 and 1750, Estienne de Lusignan, *Description de toute l'isle de Cypre* (Paris, 1580 and photo-reprint, Les Éditions L'oiseau, Famagusta, 1968):

> Pour n'oublier comment ce bestial veneneux fut extirpé du susdit Promontoire il fault noter ce qui s'ensuit: . . . le premier Duc de Cypre, fist bastir un Monastère de Moynes de l'ordre de sainct Basile en l'honneur de sainct Nicolas, et donna tout ce Promontoire à ce Monastnt tenus d'y nourrir tous les jours cent chats pour le moins, ausquels ils bailleroient quelque viande de tous les jours au matin et au soir, au son d'une petite cloche, afin qu'ils ne mangeassent pas tousjours du venin, et le reste du jour et de la nuict allassent

à la chasse de ces serpens. Mesme de notre temps ce Mona-
stère nourrissoit encore plus de quarante chats. Et de là
vient, qu'on l'appelle encores aujourdhuy le Promontoire
des Chats.

220   *Ramazan* was one of Seferis's cats.

220   *My friend, though, might well have stopped*: the allusion is to the
poet D. I. Antoniou (see note to p. 51).

223   '*On Aspalathoi . . .* ': Plato, *Republic*, 616.

225   *Rhymed Poems (1924–1953)*: this section includes all but three
of Seferis's early rhymed poems and all but two of the eight
rhymed poems that he published after *Mythistorema* (1935).
These poems are tightly rhymed in the original; some make use
of traditional forms and rhythms, including the *dekapentasylla-
vos* (see Foreword, p. xi), while others (for example, *The
Cistern*) contain intricate internal rhymes and verbal configura-
tions. We have not aspired to any sort of close formal approxi-
mation of these poems, in order to limit the distortion that such
translation would involve; their inclusion in this appendix is, in
any case, a tacit admission that our versions, compared to the
originals, are little more than bones from which the flesh has
disappeared. Indeed, we have omitted the three early poems
('Σχόλια', 'Εἰς μνήμην', and 'Δημοτικό τραγούδι') because
they did not seem to us to come over into English adequately
enough to justify their inclusion at all. We have omitted one
late rhymed poem ('Νεόφυτος ὁ ἔγκλειστος μιλά') for similar
reasons, and we have kept another ('The Jasmine') in its orig-
inal position since in this instance we have offered a formal
equivalent.

227   Epigraph: a classical phrase which can be translated literally as
'for your sake' or 'for your pleasure'.

229   Epigraph: Book III, 1,277–78. See note to p. 43.

231   The *Hydra* was a poisonous water-snake with nine heads that
merely grew in number when severed – unless cauterized, as
Heracles proved in destroying it. Also, a southern constellation
represented as a snake on maps of the heavens.

236   Epigraph: Homer, *Odyssey*, I.8–9.

237   Epigraph: a phrase from a song popular in the 1920s.

239   Epigraph: from *A Narrative of A. Gordon Pym*, Chapter 10.

245   Title: literally, 'Discourse on Love'. Cf. Plato, *Phaedrus*, 227 C.
      Epigraph: *Pythian Odes*, III.21–23.

248   *The embrace of the heavens*: the image is from the *Erotokritos* (see
      note to p. 43), as are several others in the poem.

253   *Domenikos Theotokopoulos*, born in Crete probably in 1541, is
      better known as El Greco, painter, architect and sculptor. He
      first studied in Venice and later settled in Toledo, Spain, where
      he died in 1614. The inscription cited was written by El Greco
      himself on the plan of Toledo in his picture 'View and Plan of
      Toledo' (painted *c.* 1609 and now in the Greco Museum at
      Toledo).

258   *Placed in escort to the epitaph*: in the ritual for Good Friday in the
      Orthodox Church, the entombment of Christ is re-enacted by
      carrying around the church, and the village or the district in
      which the church is situated, an image of Christ lying as
      though dead. This image is usually embroidered on a piece of
      material and the procession is known as the *epitaphios* proces-
      sion.

267   *Spring 1156*: in 1156 Renaud de Châtillon, a French adventurer
      who had married Constance, Princess of Antioch, in 1153,
      invaded Cyprus. After carrying off what gold, silver and valu-
      able vestments he could, he drove the inhabitants down to the
      shore, and they were set free only after they had paid a huge
      indemnity. Hostages taken from the leading clergy and lay
      people were held captive until the ransom was paid. See Steven
      Runciman, *A History of the Crusades* (Cambridge, 1952), II,
      348.

271   *Christodoros* (5th century A.D.) was a prolific epic poet from
      Coptus in Egypt. He wrote an epic on the Isaurian victory of
      Anastasius in 497 and versified histories of a number of cities,
      including Thessaloniki, Aphrodisias and Constantinople, now
      all lost. Apart from his two epigrams (*Palatine Anthology*
      VII.697–698), his only surviving work is an Ἔκφρασις
      (Description) on the statues decorating the Baths of Zeuxippos
      in Constantinople. See the description of the statue of Her-
      maphroditos, *Palatine Anthology* II.102–7.

# BIOGRAPHICAL DATA

THE FOLLOWING is based largely on G. P. Savidis, 'Σχεδίασμα Χρονολογίας τοῦ Γιώργου Σεφέρη' in 'Ἐποχές, Vol. VIII, December 1963.

| | |
|---|---|
| 1900 | Born to Stelios and Despo Seferiades on 29 February, in Smyrna. |
| 1914 | Moved with his family from Smyrna to Athens, where he received his secondary education. |
| 1918–24 | Studied in Paris, where he earned a degree in law. |
| 1924–5 | First visit to London. |
| 1926 | Appointed to the Greek Ministry of Foreign Affairs. Served in Athens until 1931. |
| 1931–4 | Served in the Greek Consulate in London. |
| 1934–6 | Resident in Athens. |
| 1936–8 | Consul in Koritsa, Albania. |
| 1938 | Appointed press officer to the Department of Press and Information. |
| 1941 | Married Maria Zannou. Accompanied the Greek government in exile to Crete, Egypt and finally South Africa, where he served in the Greek Embassy at Pretoria until 1942. |
| 1942–4 | Press officer to the Greek government in Cairo. |
| 1944 | Accompanied the Greek government to Italy. |
| 1945–6 | Director of the Political Bureau of the Regent Archbishop Damaskinos. |
| 1946–8 | Ministry of Foreign Affairs, Athens. |
| 1948–50 | Counsellor of Embassy in Ankara, Turkey. |
| 1951–2 | Counsellor of Embassy in London. |
| 1953–6 | Served as Ambassador to Lebanon, Syria, Jordan and Iraq. In 1953, 1954 and 1955 he visited Cyprus. |
| 1956–7 | Director of the Second Political Bureau of the Ministry of Foreign Affairs, Athens. |
| 1957 | Member of the Greek delegation to the United Nations, New York, during the discussion of the Cyprus question. |

1957–62   Ambassador to Great Britain.

1960   Hon. D. Litt. (Cantab).

1962   Foyle Award.

1962   Retired from the diplomatic service, settled in Athens.

1963   Nobel Prize for Literature.

1964   Hon. D. Litt. (Oxon).

1964   Hon. D. Philosophy (Salonika).

1965   Hon. D. Litt. (Princeton).

1966   Elected Honorary Foreign Member, American Academy of Arts and Sciences.

1966   Appointed Honorary Fellow, Modern Language Association.

1968   Member, Institute for Advanced Study, Princeton, N.J.

1969   On 20 March, issued statement condemning the Papadopoulos dictatorship.

1971   Died on 21 September, after extended hospitalization. His funeral in Athens drew a vast crowd and was linked to the protest movement against the dictatorial régime.

# INDEX OF TITLES

*Cavafy's Alexandria, Revised Edition*
by Edmund Keeley

*The Films of Theo Angelopoulos: A Cinema of Contemplation*
by Andrew Horton

*The Muslim Bonaparte: Diplomacy
and Orientalism in Ali Pasha's Greece*
by Katherine E. Fleming

THE LOCKERT LIBRARY OF POETRY IN TRANSLATION

*George Seferis: Collected Poems (1924–1955)*
translated, edited, and introduced by Edmund Keeley and Philip Sherrard

*Collected Poems of Lucio Piccolo*
translated and edited by Brian Swann and Ruth Feldman

*C.P. Cavafy: Collected Poems*
translated by Edmund Keeley and Philip Sherrard and
edited by George Savidis

*Benny Andersen: Selected Poems*
translated by Alexander Taylor

*Selected Poetry of Andrea Zanzotto*
edited and translated by Ruth Feldman and Brian Swann

*Poems of René Char*
translated and annotated by Mary Ann Caws and Jonathan Griffin

*Selected Poems of Tudor Arghezi*
translated by Michael Impey and Brian Swann

*"The Survivor" and Other Poems*
by Tadeusz Różewicz, translated and
introduced by Magnus J. Krynski and Robert A. Maguire

*"Harsh World" and Other Poems*
by Angel González, translated by Donald D. Walsh

*Ritsos in Parentheses*
translations and introduction by Edmund Keeley

*Salamander: Selected Poems of Robert Marteau*
translated by Anne Winters

*Birds and Other Relations: Selected Poetry of Dezső Tandori*
translated by Bruce Berlind

*Brocade River Poems: Selected Works of the Tang Dynasty
Courtesan Xue Tao*
translated and introduced by Jeanne Larsen

*The True Subject: Selected Poems of Faiz Ahmed Faiz*
translated by Naomi Lazard

*My Name on the Wind: Selected Poems of Diego Valeri*
translated by Michael Palma

*Aeschylus: The Suppliants*
translated by Peter Burian

*Foamy Sky: The Major Poems of Miklós Radnóti*
selected and translated by Zsuzsanna Ozsváth and Frederick Turner

*La Fontaine's Bawdy: Of Libertines, Louts, and Lechers*
translated by Norman R. Shapiro

*A Child Is Not a Knife: Selected Poems of Göran Sonnevi*
translated and edited by Rika Lesser

*George Seferis: Collected Poems, Revised Edition*
translated, edited, and introduced by Edmund Keeley
and Philip Sherrard

*C.P. Cavafy: Collected Poems, Revised Edition*
translated and introduced by Edmund Keeley and Philip Sherrard,
and edited by George Savidis

*The Late Poems of Meng Chiao*
translated and introduced by David Hinton

*Leopardi: Selected Poems*
translated and introduced by Eamon Grennan

*Through Naked Branches: Selected Poems of Tarjei Vesaas*
translated and edited by Roger Greenwald

Printed in the USA
CPSIA information can be obtained
at www.ICGtesting.com
JSHW020233170924
69848JS00003B/5

9 780691 264660